ANNE WILLAN'S
LOOK&COOK

Chocolate Desserts

ANNE WILLAN'S
LOOK&COOK

Chocolate Desserts

DORLING KINDERSLEY, INC.
NEW YORK

A DORLING KINDERSLEY BOOK

Created and Produced by
CARROLL & BROWN LIMITED
5 Lonsdale Road
London NW6 6RA

Editorial Director Jeni Wright
Editors Norma MacMillan
Stella Vayne
Art Editor Mary Staples
Designers Lyndel Donaldson
Wendy Rogers
Lucy de Rosa
Lisa Webb

First American Edition, 1992
10 9 8 7 6 5 4 3 2 1

Published in the United States by
Dorling Kindersley, Inc., 232 Madison Avenue
New York, New York 10016

Willan, Anne.
    Chocolate desserts / by Anne Willan. – 1st American ed.
    p.   cm. – (Look and cook)
    Includes index.
    ISBN 1-56458-031-8
    1. Cookery (Chocolate) 2. Desserts. I. Title. II. Title:
Chocolate desserts.   III. Series: Willan, Anne. Look and cook.
TX767. C5W55   1992
641.6'374—dc20   91-42323
                                                        CIP

Reproduced by Colourscan, Singapore
Printed and bound in Italy by A. Mondadori, Verona

CONTENTS

CHOCOLATE
THE LOOK & COOK APPROACH

Welcome to **Chocolate Desserts,** and the *Look & Cook* series. These volumes are designed to be the simplest, most informative cookbooks you'll ever own. They are the closest I can come to sharing my personal techniques for cooking my favorite recipes without actually being with you in the kitchen.

Equipment and ingredients often determine whether or not you can cook a particular dish, so *Look & Cook* illustrates everything you need at the beginning of each recipe. You'll see at a glance how long a recipe takes to cook, how many servings it makes, what the finished dish looks like, and how much preparation can be done ahead. When you start to cook, you'll find the preparation and cooking are organized into easy-to-follow steps. Each stage is color-coded and everything is shown in photographs with brief text to go with each step. You will never be in doubt as to what it is you are doing, why you are doing it, or how it should look.

EQUIPMENT

INGREDIENTS

🍽 SERVES 8   🥄 WORK TIME 25-30 MINUTES   ☕ BAKING TIME 25-30 MINUTES

I've also included helpful hints and ideas under "Anne Says." These may list an alternative ingredient or piece of equipment, or explain a certain method, or advise on mastering a particular technique. Similarly, if there is a crucial stage in a recipe when things can go wrong, I've included some warnings called "Take Care."

Many of the photographs are annotated to pinpoint why certain pieces of equipment work best, or how the food should look at that stage of cooking. Because presentation is so important, a picture of the finished dish and serving suggestions are at the end of each recipe. Many simple ideas for decoration are included, but a few, such as piped fans, will challenge the accomplished cook.

Thanks to all this information, you can't go wrong. I'll be with you every step of the way. So please, come with me into the kitchen to look, cook, and create some stunning **Chocolate Desserts.**

6

WHY CHOCOLATE?

*Whose eyes do not light up at the sight of a luscious chocolate dessert?
You may debate the merits of white versus dark chocolate, or which brand is
best, and whether the high cocoa butter content of covering chocolate (couverture)
is preferable to plainer types, but there is no disagreement that chocolate is everyone's
favorite. Indeed, it is so versatile that you might even be tempted to limit your
dessert repertoire to this fabulous flavor. Your guests will surely applaud!*

RECIPE CHOICE

No matter what its origin, a chocolate dessert needs no passport. European chocolate tortes and mousses are as eagerly received as American cakes and ice creams. Some cooks find chocolate temperamental, but once you understand how it works, you will have no trouble. In this volume, I'll be showing you how to make perfect cake batters, fillings, icings, and garnishes. Chocolate decorations, which offer so much variety, are featured in many recipes. There is something for everyone – from light, airy soufflés and chocolate sorbet to sumptuously rich cakes and crispy chocolate crème brûlée.

CHOCOLATE CAKES

For everyday occasions plain chocolate cakes are ideal. *Chocolate Orange Pound Cake*: Flavored with homemade candied orange peel and topped with a light orange icing. *Chocolate Orange Marble Pound Cake*: Chocolate orange and plain orange batters are swirled to create a marbled effect. *Speckled Chocolate Cake*: Curls of dark chocolate hide a moist cake speckled with nuggets of chopped chocolate. *Chocolate Butterfly Cakes*: A children's treat; tops of chocolate chip cupcakes settle on filling to resemble butterfly wings.

Well-beloved European favorites are among my classic choices. *Chocolate Walnut Torte*: Rich and laden with ground nuts and dark chocolate, topped with Chantilly cream. *Chocolate Almond Torte:* Another flourless cake, this dense almond torte is topped with a lattice of sprinkled confectioners' sugar and cocoa. *Sachertorte:* The world-famous rich chocolate cake hailing from Austria.

Chocolate Raspberry Torte: Served with fresh raspberries, this lavish version of Sachertorte has a glaze of raspberry jam under silky icing. *Black Forest Cake*: From the Black Forest of Germany comes this cake flavored with kirsch, layered with Chantilly cream and dark cherries. *Black Forest Strip Cake*: When shaped in a rectangle, Black Forest cake is easy to slice. *Chocolate Praline Cake:* Chocolate layer cake with rum syrup and crunchy caramel-almond praline.

Roulades or roll cakes feature a variety of fillings. *Chocolate Chestnut Roll*: A winter filling of chestnut, whipped cream and dark rum. *Chocolate Strawberry Cream Cake*: A must with fresh, sweet summer strawberries. *Chocolate Nut Cream Cake with Caramel Sauce*: Hazelnuts and caramel pair deliciously in another version of a chocolate roll.

Now for the ultimate chocolate cakes. *Chocolate Orange Truffle Cake*: Rich, thick ganache flavored with Grand Marnier crowns a light sponge cake. *Chocolate Coffee Truffle Cake*: Chocolate addicts beware! *Checkerboard Cake with Chocolate Ganache*: A surprise awaits beneath the rich ganache frosting of this eye-catching chocolate and vanilla checkerboard cake. *Apricot Checkerboard Cake*: Apricots make a tart-sweet, golden sauce, providing a delicious contrast with this checkerboard cake.

A superlative finish with a trio of chocolate cheesecakes. *Chocolate Marble Cheesecake*: Swirls of chocolate and plain cheesecake fillings in a delectable dessert. *All-Chocolate Cheesecake*: For chocolate purists. *White Chocolate Cheesecake*: A cream-colored mixture with white chocolate fills this cheesecake.

CHOCOLATE DESSERTS

Chocolate-flavored custards and creams are great for special occasions. *Chocolate Crème Brûlée:* The classic crème brûlée with a chocolate accent. *Chocolate Crème Brûlée with Raspberries:* Fresh raspberries are concealed with the chocolate cream under the topping of caramelized sugar. *Chocolate Mousse with Hazelnuts and Whiskey:* Who can say "no" to chocolate mousse, with the nutty zip of hazelnuts, and whiskey. *Double-Chocolate Mousse:* Chunks of white chocolate contrast with smooth dark chocolate mousse.

Mousse and more make three great desserts. *Black and White Chocolate Mousse Towers:* Disks of dark chocolate layered with white chocolate mousse and blueberries, form individual towers in pools of raspberry coulis. *Dark Chocolate Whiskey Mousse Towers:* The filling of dark chocolate mousse laced with whiskey is spiked with plump blueberries. *Marbled Black and White Chocolate Mousse Towers:* Here dark chocolate squares are feathered with white chocolate and layered with white chocolate mousse and delicious fresh raspberries.

Hot desserts are also impressive. *Chocolate Soufflé:* Light as air and deliciously rich. *Individual Chocolate Soufflés:* Single serving portions of an all-time favorite. *Amaretto Chocolate Soufflé:* Almond cookies soaked in almond liqueur are hidden in the center of this soufflé. *Steamed Mexican Chocolate Pudding with Apricot Sauce:* This classic steamed pudding is spiced with cinnamon and cloves and served with an apricot sauce. *Steamed Mexican Chocolate Pudding with Chocolate Sauce:* The same spicy pudding with a hot, dark chocolate sauce.

Chocolate and pastry combined create elegant desserts. *Chocolate and Pear Tartlets:* A great fruit and chocolate match, with a topping of thinly sliced fresh pear. *Chocolate and Apple Tartlets:* Chunks of apple, sautéed with sugar and cinnamon, top the chocolate in these little tarts. *Profiteroles with Chocolate Ice Cream:* Puffs of choux pastry are filled with rich chocolate ice cream, topped with a contrasting hot chocolate sauce. *Chocolate Ice Cream Swans:* Choux pastry baked in elegant swan shapes, filled with ice cream and floating on a lake of rich chocolate sauce. *Choux Chantilly Ring:* Chocolate sauce accompanies a ring of choux pastry filled with airy Chantilly cream.

Incredibly dark and delicious are the following. *Chocolate Charlotte:* Half fudge, half cake, this intense chocolate mold swathed in Chantilly cream is the perfect winter treat. *Small Chocolate Charlottes:* A charlotte per person, for devout chocolate lovers.

ICED CHOCOLATE DESSERTS

Enjoy the ice creams and sorbets on their own or use to top or fill other treats. *Chocolate Ice Cream:* Rich and delicious, loved by one and all. *Chocolate Indulgence Ice Cream:* An indulgence indeed! *Chocolate Praline Ice Cream:* The nutty crunch of praline with the sweet smoothness of chocolate ice cream. *Chocolate Mocha Sorbet:* Coffee adds delicious intensity to chocolate sorbet. *Chocolate Sorbet:* The impact of this ultra-simple sorbet, made with unsweetened chocolate, is a surprise.

Some eye-catching desserts to end. *Chocolate and Apricot Bombe:* Elegant molded dessert of chocolate ice cream, filled with a creamy apricot mixture and served with chocolate fudge sauce. *Bombe Royale:* What could be better than jelly roll, chocolate ice cream and the tang of apricot brandy! *Chef Ferré's Frozen Tri-Chocolate Terrine:* From a top Paris pastry chef comes this iced terrine with layers of white, milk, and dark chocolate, served on a pool of mint custard sauce. *Tri-Chocolate Terrine on Strawberry Coulis:* The same creamy layered dessert, offset by fresh strawberry coulis.

EQUIPMENT

I've deliberately chosen these recipes to require little in the way of special equipment. However, the cakes do need specific pans of certain shapes and sizes. It is not advisable to change the size of the cake pans because the batter will not bake correctly. The cheesecake uses a springform pan, while the chocolate terrines and bombes call for special molds. Many of the desserts can be made in individual versions so you will find small and large ramekins useful, but custard cups or ovenproof *demitasse* cups can be substituted. A pastry bag and a selection of different tubes are important for piping some of the fillings and decorations. An ice-cream maker is necessary for the ice creams and sorbet.

INGREDIENTS

Chocolate takes kindly to a wide variety of other ingredients. Toasted and ground nuts add texture and flavor to chocolate cakes and fillings. Cream adds lightness and a contrast of color, while coffee transforms chocolate into mocha.

Juicy berries – raspberries, strawberries, blueberries, and their cousins – are classic accompaniments, often as a coulis or sauce. Fresh fruits – notably oranges, apricots, cherries, pears, and apples – are often paired with chocolate or used in a delicious jam glaze.

Another way to balance the richness of chocolate is by adding rum, whiskey or brandy, or liqueurs, such as Grand Marnier or kirsch.

TECHNIQUES

Working with chocolate needs care, but once you have mastered a handful of techniques your repertoire of chocolate desserts will expand quickly.

The building blocks for many of my recipes are important basics such as chopping, grating, and melting chocolate. Melted chocolate is also the foundation for a wide variety of decorative techniques – for piping shapes, such as fans, and for spreading to make leaves. "How-To" boxes will help you master them. Melted chocolate can be spread flat to make a ribbon for wrapping around a cake, or to cut into an assortment of shapes – squares, triangles, coins, and disks.

To improve the gloss of many of these decorations, professionals often temper chocolate, and here I show you an easy and reliable method.

Because so many of the chocolate recipes call for garnishes and because chocolate decorations are so popular with other types of desserts, there is further information on making chocolate decorations, with photographs of the finished results, in Chocolate Know-How.

As with the other volumes in this series, I have also included techniques for the other ingredients that are used in these chocolate recipes. For instance, you will find out how to make Chantilly cream, caramel cream sauce, berry coulis and jam glaze; how to toast and skin nuts; how to make candied orange peel, and make and crush praline; how to fold mixtures together; how to separate eggs and whisk egg whites. There are instructions for making a paper piping cone, as well as for filling a pastry bag, for lining a round cake pan, and lining and flouring a loaf pan.

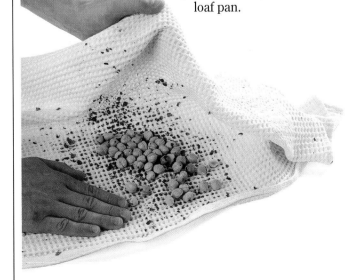

9

CHOCOLATE WALNUT TORTE

EQUIPMENT

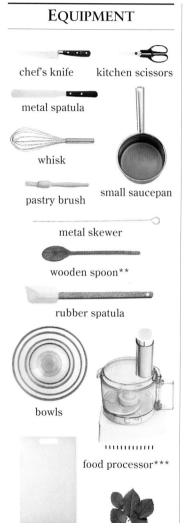

chef's knife   kitchen scissors

metal spatula

whisk

pastry brush   small saucepan

metal skewer

wooden spoon**

rubber spatula

bowls   food processor***

chopping board   20-25 rose leaves

9-inch springform pan   plate

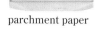

parchment paper

** electric mixer can also be used
*** blender can also be used

A torte in the true tradition of flourless cakes, this Chocolate Walnut Torte is based on ground walnuts and chocolate, lightened with meringue. The batter is baked slowly in a low oven so the edges of the cake do not dry and the end result is beautifully moist. The Chantilly cream and piped chocolate add a luxurious finishing touch.

GETTING AHEAD

The torte can be prepared and baked up to 1 week ahead and kept in an airtight container. Make the Chantilly cream and add the chocolate topping not more than 2 hours before serving.

plus cooling and chilling time

SHOPPING LIST

	butter and flour for pan
12 oz	semisweet chocolate
1 ²/₃ cups	walnut pieces
4	eggs
¹/₂ cup	unsalted butter
1 cup	sugar
	For the Chantilly cream
1 cup	heavy cream
1 tbsp	sugar
¹/₂ tsp	vanilla extract

INGREDIENTS

semisweet chocolate   walnut pieces

eggs   heavy cream

unsalted butter   vanilla extract

sugar

ANNE SAYS

"Unsalted butter is important in pastries and cake fillings because its flavor is sweet and rich. Salted butter gives a sharper flavor."

ORDER OF WORK

1   **MAKE THE TORTE BATTER**

2   **BAKE THE TORTE AND MAKE THE CHOCOLATE LEAVES**

3   **FINISH THE TORTE**

HOW TO LINE A ROUND CAKE PAN

Lining a cake pan with parchment paper ensures that the cake will not stick. If the batter is rich, the pan should also be floured so that any excess butter is absorbed.

1 Melt 2-3 tbsp butter and brush inside the pan with an even coating, making sure the bottom and top edges are covered.

2 Fold a square of parchment paper in quarters, then in triangular eighths. Hold the point of the paper triangle over the center of the pan and cut the paper even with the inside edge. Unfold the paper and press it onto the bottom of the pan. Butter the paper.

3 If directed in the recipe, flour the pan: Sprinkle in 2-3 tbsp flour, then turn and shake the pan so that the flour evenly coats the bottom and side. Tap the pan to remove all excess flour.

1 MAKE THE TORTE BATTER

1 Heat the oven to 300°F. Butter, line, and flour the pan (see box, left). Chop 3 ½ oz of the chocolate and grind with half of the walnuts in the food processor or blender. Repeat with another 3 ½ oz chocolate and the remaining nuts. (If using a blender, grind the chocolate and nuts in 4 batches.)

ANNE SAYS
"For a finer texture, grind the nuts in a rotary hand grater. Then mix the nuts with the chocolate after it has been chopped."

3 Add the egg yolks one by one, beating thoroughly after each addition.

2 Separate the eggs (see box, page 12). With the wooden spoon, cream the butter. Add three-quarters of the sugar and beat until light and fluffy, 2-3 minutes.

Add ground chocolate and walnut mixture to creamed mixture all at once

4 Stir the ground chocolate and walnut mixture into the batter using the rubber spatula.

5 Whisk the egg whites until stiff. Sprinkle in the remaining sugar and continue whisking until glossy.

6 Add the meringue to the chocolate mixture and fold them together using the rubber spatula.

2 BAKE THE TORTE AND MAKE THE CHOCOLATE LEAVES

1 Transfer the torte batter to the prepared pan and smooth the top with the spatula.

2 Bake until the skewer inserted in the center of the torte comes out clean, 60-70 minutes.

3 Let the torte cool completely in the pan. When the cake is completely cold, unsnap the hinge on the side of the cake pan and lift it gently away from the cake.

ANNE SAYS
"The torte is so delicate, it is best served still on the base of the pan."

4 Make the chocolate leaves: Melt 4 oz of the remaining chocolate. Using the pastry brush, spread chocolate on the shiny side of the rose leaves in a thin, even layer, leaving a little of the stems exposed. Set the leaves on a plate and let cool, then refrigerate until set. With the tips of your fingers, peel the leaves away from the chocolate.

HOW TO SEPARATE EGGS

Eggs are easy to separate by using the shell. However, if an egg is contaminated with salmonella, bacteria can cling to the shell and spread. Alternative methods are filtering the white through your fingers or using an egg separator.

1 **To separate an egg with the shell:** Crack the egg at its broadest point by tapping it against a bowl. With 2 thumbs, break it open, letting some white slip over the edge of the shell into the bowl.

2 Tip yolk from one half of the shell to the other, detaching the remaining white from the yolk. If some yolk slips into the white, remove it with the shell. To remove white threads, pinch them against side of shell with your fingertips.

To separate an egg with your fingers: Crack the egg into a bowl. Hold your cupped fingers over another bowl and let the white fall through them, leaving the yolk.

3 FINISH THE TORTE

1 Make the Chantilly cream: Whip the cream in a bowl set in a larger bowl of ice water until soft peaks form. Add the sugar and vanilla and whip until soft peaks form again.

2 With the metal spatula, spread the cream evenly over the top and side of the cake. Place the cake on a serving plate and chill about 1 hour.

3 For the topping, chop the remaining 1 oz chocolate and melt it in a bowl set in a saucepan of hot water. Make a paper piping cone and fill with the chocolate. Pipe the chocolate lightly over the cake in a linear design. Clean the plate if necessary, and arrange the chocolate leaves around the edge.

ANNE SAYS
"Rather than piping on the chocolate, you can drizzle it over the cake with a teaspoon."

!○! TO SERVE
Cut the cake into wedges and place on individual plates. Arrange a few chocolate leaves on each plate.

Piped chocolate topping is simple to do but looks very special

Chocolate leaves are a beautiful decoration for any cake or dessert

CHOCOLATE ALMOND TORTE
Almonds add crunch to this variation of Chocolate Walnut Torte.

1 Replace the walnuts with the same amount of whole blanched almonds. Toast the almonds before grinding, and make the cake as directed.
2 Omit the Chantilly cream and chocolate topping and decorate the cake as follows: Cut four to five $3/4$-inch-wide strips of light cardboard and lay them on top of the cake. Sprinkle with confectioners' sugar. Carefully lift off the strips and discard the excess sugar.

3 Lay the strips back on the cake to make a diagonal lattice on the sugar bands. Sift cocoa powder generously over the top, and carefully lift off the cardboard strips, discarding the excess cocoa powder.

CHOCOLATE ORANGE POUND CAKE

🍴 SERVES 6-8 🥣 WORK TIME ABOUT 2 HOURS* 🍲 BAKING TIME 50-60 MINUTES

EQUIPMENT

saucepans

strainer

kitchen scissors

8 ½- x 4 ½- x 3-inch loaf pan

ovenproof plate

chef's knife

small knife

pastry brush

electric mixer

slotted spoon

bowls

wire rack

chopping board

tray

juicer

wooden spoon

parchment paper

rubber spatula

metal skewer

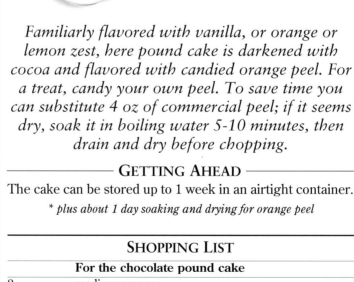
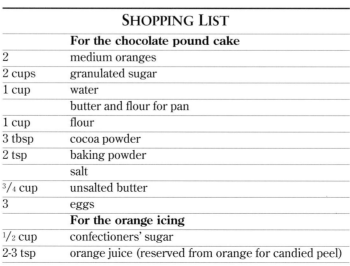

Familiarly flavored with vanilla, or orange or lemon zest, here pound cake is darkened with cocoa and flavored with candied orange peel. For a treat, candy your own peel. To save time you can substitute 4 oz of commercial peel; if it seems dry, soak it in boiling water 5-10 minutes, then drain and dry before chopping.

GETTING AHEAD

The cake can be stored up to 1 week in an airtight container.

* plus about 1 day soaking and drying for orange peel

INGREDIENTS

flour

oranges

confectioners' sugar

eggs

unsalted butter

baking powder

granulated sugar

cocoa powder

ORDER OF WORK

1 MAKE THE CHOCOLATE POUND CAKE

2 MAKE THE ORANGE ICING

3 ICE AND DECORATE THE CAKE

SHOPPING LIST

For the chocolate pound cake	
2	medium oranges
2 cups	granulated sugar
1 cup	water
	butter and flour for pan
1 cup	flour
3 tbsp	cocoa powder
2 tsp	baking powder
	salt
³/₄ cup	unsalted butter
3	eggs
For the orange icing	
½ cup	confectioners' sugar
2-3 tsp	orange juice (reserved from orange for candied peel)

1 MAKE THE CHOCOLATE POUND CAKE

1 Make the candied orange peel (see box, page 18) using the oranges, 1 cup of the sugar, and the water. Reserve several pieces for decoration, and finely chop the rest. Heat the oven to 350° F. Butter, line, and flour the loaf pan (see box, page 17).

2 Sift the flour into a medium bowl with the cocoa powder, baking powder, and a pinch of salt. Set aside.

Butter and sugar mixture will gradually lighten as sugar dissolves

3 With the electric mixer, cream the butter. Add the remaining 1 cup sugar and continue beating until light and fluffy, about 2-3 minutes.

4 Add the eggs to the butter and sugar mixture one by one, beating thoroughly with the electric mixer after each addition.

ANNE SAYS
"If the mixture begins to separate while adding the eggs, heat the bowl gently over hot water."

Set bowl on dampened dish towel to hold it steady while you beat

Mix in candied peel quickly and lightly

5 With the rubber spatula, stir the finely chopped candied orange peel evenly into the batter.

6 Stir the flour mixture into the batter until just mixed.

7 Transfer the batter to the prepared loaf pan. Tap the pan on the table to level the surface of the batter and knock out large air bubbles.

Metal skewer is used to test if cake is done; wooden toothpick could also be used

8 Bake the pound cake in the heated oven until it shrinks slightly from the sides of the pan and the skewer inserted in the center comes out clean, 50-60 minutes. While the cake is baking, make the orange icing (see page 17).

Indentation in center is characteristic of pound cake

HOW TO LINE AND FLOUR A LOAF PAN

Lining a cake pan with parchment paper keeps the cake from sticking to the inside of the pan. Flouring the pan also ensures that any excess butter will be absorbed from rich batters.

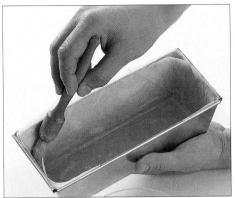

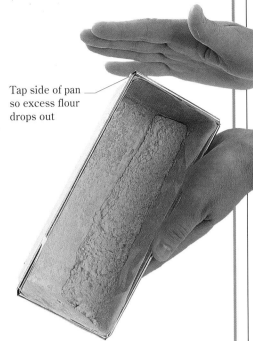

Tap side of pan so excess flour drops out

1 On the work surface, lay a rectangle of parchment paper 6 inches wider and 6 inches longer than the base of the loaf pan. Set the pan in the middle of the paper. With the scissors, snip diagonally from the corners of the paper to the corners of the pan.

2 Melt 2-3 tbsp of butter and brush the inside of the pan with an even coating, making sure that the bottom and top edges are covered. Press the paper into the pan, tucking in the overlaps to fit into the corners. Trim the paper even with the top edges. Butter the paper.

3 To flour the pan, sprinkle in 2-3 tbsp flour, and turn the pan so that the flour evenly coats the bottom and sides. Tap to remove excess flour.

2 MAKE THE ORANGE ICING

Orange icing should have easy pouring consistency

1 Sift the confectioners' sugar into a small bowl and stir in enough of the orange juice to make a soft paste.

ANNE SAYS
"Adjust the consistency of the icing by adding more confectioners' sugar if the icing is too thin or more orange juice if it is too thick."

2 Set the bowl in a saucepan of hot, not simmering, water, and heat until the icing is warm and will pour easily from the spoon. Keep the icing warm.

HOW TO MAKE CANDIED ORANGE PEEL

Fruits are candied, or crystallized, by being cooked in concentrated sugar syrup until translucent. Some fruits, in particular citrus peel and slices, can be candied at home easily. They make a tangy addition to cakes.

1 Score the orange peel lengthwise into quarters with a small knife, then strip away the peel and pith with your fingers.

ANNE SAYS
"Before peeling the oranges, roll them gently on the work surface to loosen the peel."

3 Cut one orange in half and squeeze the juice; reserve for the icing.

2 Cut the peel into ¼-inch-wide strips using a chef's knife.

4 Heat the sugar with the water in a saucepan until dissolved, then bring the syrup just to a boil. Put the strips of peel in the syrup.

Use slotted spoon to transfer peel from pan to rack

Put tray under rack to catch drips of syrup

5 Press a circle of parchment paper over the peel and weigh it down with a plate so the strips are immersed in syrup. Bring the syrup slowly to a simmer, taking 10-12 minutes, then poach until tender to the bite, about 1 hour.

6 Take the saucepan from the heat and let the peel soak in the syrup at room temperature 24 hours. Transfer the peel to a rack placed over a tray and let dry, 3-5 hours.

3 ICE AND DECORATE THE CAKE

1 Remove the cake from the oven. Run the small knife around the sides of the warm cake to loosen it, then transfer it to the rack, with the tray below to catch the drips from the icing. Strip the paper from the cake.

Pour icing slowly over cake to coat evenly

2 Pour the warm icing over the cake. Decorate the top with the reserved pieces of candied orange peel. Leave until the cake is cool and the icing has set.

TO SERVE
Transfer the cake to a serving plate and cut into thin slices.

Pieces of candied orange peel make colorful contrast on top of dark brown cake

VARIATION

CHOCOLATE ORANGE MARBLE POUND CAKE

This attractive variation adds a swirl of plain orange batter to Chocolate Orange Pound Cake.

1 Make the candied orange peel as directed, then chop all of it.
2 Sift the flour with the baking powder and salt and divide evenly between 2 bowls. Sift 3 tbsp cocoa powder into one of the bowls.
3 Continue making the cake batter as directed in steps 3, 4, and 5, then divide it in half. Stir the cocoa mixture into one portion and the plain flour mixture into the other portion.
4 Pour the plain batter into the prepared loaf pan.

5 Pour the chocolate batter over the plain batter in the pan.
6 Using the tip of a knife, swirl the batters together in a marbled pattern, taking care not to overmix them or the marbled effect will be lost.
7 Bake and ice the cake as directed.

CHOCOLATE MARBLE CHEESECAKE

 SERVES 8-10   WORK TIME 35-40 MINUTES* BAKING TIME 50-60 MINUTES

EQUIPMENT

8-inch springform pan

metal spoon

pastry brush

table knife   food processor

bowls

chopping board

chef's knife

electric mixer

small knife

saucepans

rubber spatula

wooden spoon

INGREDIENTS

graham crackers

unsalted butter

semisweet chocolate

sugar

cream cheese

vanilla extract

eggs

This all-American favorite has swirls of plain and chocolate cheesecake fillings flavored with vanilla in a crumbled graham cracker crust. The marbled filling is dense and rich, making it an ideal dinner party dessert.

GETTING AHEAD
The cheesecake can be made up to 3 days ahead and kept refrigerated; the flavor will mellow.

* plus 5-9 hours cooling and chilling time

SHOPPING LIST

	For the crust
	melted butter for pan
10	whole graham crackers, weighing 5 oz
1/3 cup	unsalted butter
	For the cheesecake filling
5 oz	semisweet chocolate
1 lb	cream cheese, softened
3/4 cup	sugar
1 tsp	vanilla extract
2	eggs

ORDER OF WORK

1 MAKE THE CRUST

2 MAKE THE CHEESECAKE FILLING

3 MARBLE AND BAKE THE CHEESECAKE

1 MAKE THE CRUST

Brush melted butter thickly over side and bottom of pan

1 Generously brush the inside of the pan with melted butter and chill it.

Melted butter is best for brushing on inside of cake pans because it spreads evenly

2 Grind the graham crackers to fine crumbs in the food processor; transfer to a bowl. Melt the butter in a small saucepan; add to the crumbs.

ANNE SAYS
"As an alternative to grinding the graham crackers in a food processor, put them in a plastic bag and crush them with a rolling pin."

3 Stir with the wooden spoon until all the crumbs are moistened with melted butter.

Spread crumb crust evenly, pressing with back of metal spoon

4 Press the crumb mixture evenly over the bottom and up the side of the prepared pan. Chill until firm, 30-60 minutes.

HOW TO MELT CHOCOLATE

Chocolate should be melted carefully because it may scorch or harden if overheated. It is also important that the container is uncovered and dry because any water or steam in contact with the chocolate may cause it to "seize." Once the chocolate begins to melt, stir it occasionally until melted and smooth, then remove it from the heat. There are a number of methods for melting chocolate. A double boiler is good; so, too, are the methods described here. Some cooks use a microwave oven: 2 oz chopped semisweet chocolate takes about 2 minutes on Medium power.

Melt chopped chocolate in a glass bowl set in a pan of hot, not simmering, water (a water bath).

Alternatively, spread chopped chocolate on an ovenproof plate and melt it over a pan of boiling water.

ANNE SAYS
"If the chocolate seizes during melting, stir in vegetable shortening or oil 1 teaspoon at a time until smooth again."

2 MAKE THE CHEESECAKE FILLING

1 Heat the oven to 350° F. Cut the chocolate into large chunks. Chop them with the chef's knife, or in the food processor using the pulse button. Melt the chocolate (see box, left) and let cool.

2 Beat the cream cheese until smooth with the electric mixer, 2-3 minutes, or you can use the wooden spoon. Add the sugar and vanilla and beat just until smooth.

3 Add the eggs one by one, beating well after each addition.

Beat one egg in thoroughly before adding next

4 Pour half of the filling into the prepared crust.

5 Mix the cooled melted chocolate into the remaining filling.

3 MARBLE AND BAKE THE CHEESECAKE

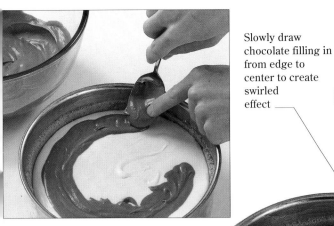

1 Slowly spoon a ring of the chocolate filling over the plain filling.

2 Using the table knife, swirl the fillings together to make a marbled pattern. Take care not to over-mix or the marbled effect will be lost. Bake the cheesecake in the heated oven until the sides are set but the center remains soft, 50-60 minutes. Turn off the oven and leave the cheesecake in the cooling-down oven until completely cool. Refrigerate at least 4 hours.

ANNE SAYS
"It is important to cool the cheesecake slowly in the oven or it will crack."

Chocolate and vanilla fillings are swirled together to create marbled effect

Slowly draw chocolate filling in from edge to center to create swirled effect

🍴 **TO SERVE**
Run the small knife around the side of the cheesecake to loosen it, remove the side of the pan, and transfer the cheesecake to a serving plate.

ANNE SAYS
"If the crust crumbles, press the crumbs back into the side."

Graham cracker crust is rich and buttery

VARIATIONS

ALL-CHOCOLATE CHEESECAKE

A thoroughly chocolate version of Chocolate Marble Cheesecake.

1 Make the crust as directed.
2 Chop and melt 10 oz semisweet chocolate.
3 Prepare the filling as directed, using only 1/2 cup sugar. Stir in the cooled, melted chocolate after the eggs.
4 Pour the filling into the prepared crust and bake as directed.

WHITE CHOCOLATE CHEESECAKE

Another version of Chocolate Marble Cheesecake – all in white.

1 Make the crust as directed.
2 Chop and melt 8 oz white chocolate.
3 Prepare the filling as directed, using only 1/2 cup sugar. Stir in the cooled, melted white chocolate after the eggs.
4 Pour the filling into the prepared crust and bake as directed.

SPECKLED CHOCOLATE CAKE

 SERVES 8   WORK TIME 30-35 MINUTES*   BAKING TIME ABOUT 50 MINUTES

EQUIPMENT

- electric mixer
- 8-inch round cake pan
- small knife
- chef's knife**
- kitchen scissors
- bowls
- vegetable peeler
- pastry brush
- saucepan
- whisk
- strainers
- metal spatula
- wooden spoon
- rubber spatula
- dish towel
- wire rack
- cardboard
- parchment paper

**food processor can also be used

This moist cake, laden with little pieces of chocolate, was created by master French Chef Fernand Point. The chopped chocolate should be slightly granular and a food processor gives the ideal texture, or use a chef's knife.

GETTING AHEAD

The cake keeps well in an airtight container up to 3 days. Frost it not more than 2 hours before serving.

* plus cooling time

SHOPPING LIST

	For the cake batter	
	butter for pan	
¹/₂ cup	unsalted butter	
4	eggs	
1¹/₄ cups	granulated sugar	
4 oz	semisweet chocolate	
1 cup	flour	
	For the chocolate frosting	
6 oz	unsweetened chocolate	
³/₄ cup	butter	
1¹/₂ cups	confectioners' sugar	
	To finish	
3 oz	bar semisweet chocolate	
	confectioners' sugar	

INGREDIENTS

semisweet and unsweetened chocolate   eggs

confectioners' sugar

butter   flour

granulated sugar

chocolate bar

ORDER OF WORK

1 MAKE THE CAKE BATTER

2 BAKE THE CAKE

3 MAKE THE CHOCOLATE FROSTING

4 FINISH THE CAKE

1 MAKE THE CAKE BATTER

1 Heat the oven to 350° F. Butter the cake pan and line the bottom with parchment paper. Butter the paper. Put the unsalted butter in a small bowl and set it in the saucepan half filled with hot water.

Warmed butter should be pourable but not oily

2 Warm the butter, stirring occasionally, until it is soft enough to pour. Remove from the heat and let cool slightly.

Gradually add sugar to egg yolks while beating with electric mixer

3 Separate the eggs. Beat the egg yolks with about two-thirds of the sugar until light and the mixture leaves a ribbon trail when the beaters are lifted, 3-5 minutes.

4 In a separate bowl, whisk the egg whites until stiff. Sprinkle in the remaining sugar and continue whisking until glossy to make a light meringue, about 20 seconds.

5 Add the softened butter to the egg yolk mixture and stir in gently.

6 Cut the chocolate into large chunks. Chop them with the chef's knife, or in a food processor using the pulse button.

Lift egg yolk mixture up and over chopped chocolate until speckled

7 Stir the chopped chocolate into the egg yolk mixture.

8 Sift about one-third of the flour into the chocolate mixture. Add about one-third of the meringue and fold them together as lightly as possible.

Use rubber spatula to fold mixtures gently together

9 Add the remaining flour and meringue in the same way in 2 more batches.

ANNE SAYS

"If the ingredients are folded together gently, air will be retained in the batter and the finished cake will be light."

2 BAKE THE CAKE

1 Pour the cake batter into the prepared pan. Bake the cake in the heated oven until it has shrunk slightly from the side of the pan, about 50 minutes.

After pouring batter into cake pan, tap pan on work surface so top of batter is level

2 Remove the cake from the oven. Run the small knife carefully around the edge of the cake to loosen it from the pan.

ANNE SAYS

"It can be hard to tell when the cake is done because the crisp top will be cracked and will not spring back when pressed with a fingertip. If in doubt, leave it in the oven longer."

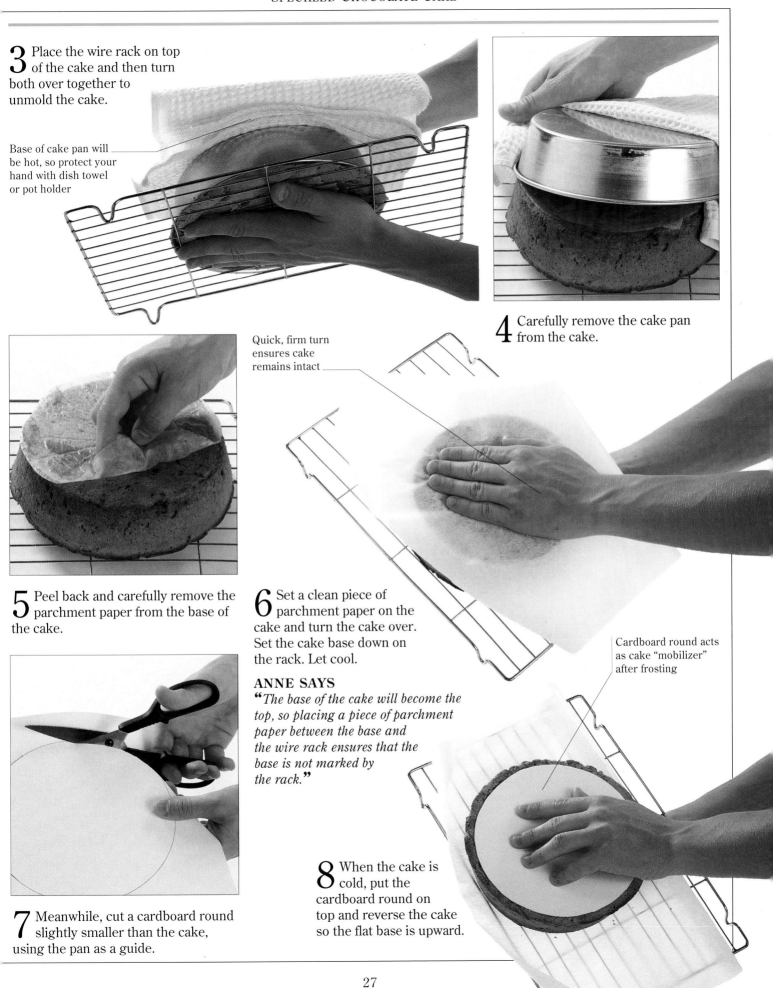

3 Place the wire rack on top of the cake and then turn both over together to unmold the cake.

Base of cake pan will be hot, so protect your hand with dish towel or pot holder

4 Carefully remove the cake pan from the cake.

Quick, firm turn ensures cake remains intact

5 Peel back and carefully remove the parchment paper from the base of the cake.

6 Set a clean piece of parchment paper on the cake and turn the cake over. Set the cake base down on the rack. Let cool.

ANNE SAYS
"*The base of the cake will become the top, so placing a piece of parchment paper between the base and the wire rack ensures that the base is not marked by the rack.*"

Cardboard round acts as cake "mobilizer" after frosting

7 Meanwhile, cut a cardboard round slightly smaller than the cake, using the pan as a guide.

8 When the cake is cold, put the cardboard round on top and reverse the cake so the flat base is upward.

3 MAKE THE CHOCOLATE FROSTING

1 Chop the chocolate, and melt it in a bowl set in the pan of hot water. Let cool slightly.

2 Meanwhile, using the wooden spoon, work the butter until it becomes soft and smooth.

3 Sift the confectioners' sugar and add it to the butter.

4 Beat the mixture well until it becomes light and creamy.

HOW TO MAKE CHOCOLATE CURLS

It is easiest to form curls from a bar of chocolate, although only a small portion of the bar may be needed. Covering chocolate (couverture) is easiest to shave, but semisweet and milk chocolate can also be used if preferred.

The chocolate should be at room temperature (about 70° F). Holding the bar at an angle, use a vegetable peeler to shave curls from the edge onto parchment paper.

Whisk quickly in warm place to keep chocolate fluid

Folded damp dish towel placed underneath bowl will prevent skidding

5 Add the melted chocolate to the creamy butter and sugar mixture, whisking quickly as you pour in the chocolate.

ANNE SAYS
"Prepare the frosting in a warm place because it sets quickly."

6 Pour about half of the frosting on top of the cake and spread it evenly over the top and side with the metal spatula. Dip the spatula in hot water, dry it quickly, and smooth the top and side of the cake.

4 FINISH THE CAKE

1 Make the chocolate curls using the 3 oz bar semisweet chocolate (see box, page 28). Using the metal spatula, lift the curls and sprinkle them on top of the cake.

Tap spatula to release any curls that stick

2 Sift confectioners' sugar evenly over the chocolate curls. Transfer the cake to a serving plate.

Chocolate curls are a simple but effective garnish

Chocolate frosting covers any unevenness in cake

CHOCOLATE BUTTERFLY CAKES

Hollowed cupcakes are filled with chocolate frosting and the tops are split to form "wings." Children love to make these small speckled chocolate cupcakes take flight.

1 Line 12 muffin tins with cupcake papers. Prepare the cake batter as directed. Spoon the batter into the cupcake papers, filling them three-quarters full. Bake the cakes until they are risen in the center and firm to the touch, 15-20 minutes. Remove from the oven, lift out of muffin tins, and place on a wire rack; let cool.
2 Make the chocolate frosting.

3 With a small knife, slice a deep cone from each of the cupcakes and cut each cone in half. Fill the hollows with the frosting, using a pastry bag and star tube if you like. Arrange the cut halves on top to resemble butterfly wings. Sift over a little confectioners' sugar and serve.

SACHERTORTE

 SERVES 8-10   WORK TIME 35-40 MINUTES* BAKING TIME 1-1¼ HOURS

EQUIPMENT

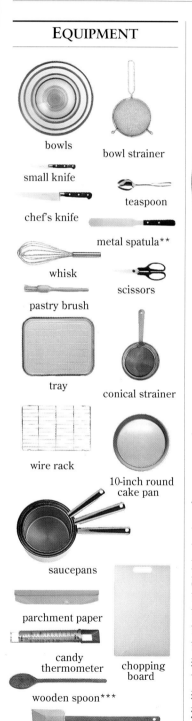

bowls

bowl strainer

small knife

teaspoon

chef's knife

metal spatula**

whisk

scissors

pastry brush

tray

conical strainer

wire rack

10-inch round
cake pan

saucepans

parchment paper

candy
thermometer

chopping
board

wooden spoon***

rubber spatula

**pastry scraper can also be used
***electric mixer can also be used

INGREDIENTS

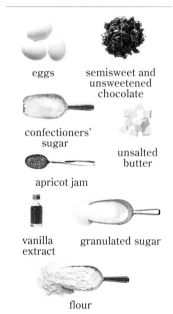

eggs

semisweet and
unsweetened
chocolate

confectioners'
sugar

unsalted
butter

apricot jam

vanilla
extract

granulated sugar

flour

The world-famous chocolate cake from Sacher's pastry shop in Vienna is embossed with the name "Sacher," which accounts for its renown.

GETTING AHEAD

The cake can be baked, iced, and stored up to 1 week in an airtight container.

* plus cooling time

SHOPPING LIST

For the chocolate cake	
	butter and flour for pan
4 oz	semisweet chocolate
6	eggs
½ cup	unsalted butter
1 cup	confectioners' sugar
½ tsp	vanilla extract
½ cup	granulated sugar
¾ cup	flour
For the apricot jam glaze	
¾ cup	apricot jam
3-4 tbsp	water
For the chocolate icing	
8 oz	unsweetened chocolate
1¼ cups	granulated sugar
½ cup	water

ORDER OF WORK

1 **PREPARE AND BAKE THE CHOCOLATE CAKE**

2 **MAKE THE APRICOT JAM GLAZE; USE TO COAT THE CAKE**

3 **MAKE THE CHOCOLATE ICING AND ICE THE CAKE**

1 PREPARE AND BAKE THE CHOCOLATE CAKE

1 Heat the oven to 350° F. Butter the cake pan, line the bottom with parchment paper, butter the paper, and flour the pan. Cut the chocolate into large chunks. Chop them with the chef's knife, or in a food processor using the pulse button. Melt in a bowl set in a saucepan with hot water.

Stir chocolate with rubber spatula while it melts to ensure smooth texture

2 Separate the eggs. With the wooden spoon, cream the butter. Add the confectioners' sugar and vanilla extract and continue beating until light and fluffy, 2-3 minutes.

3 Add the egg yolks one by one, beating well after each addition. Stir in the melted chocolate.

Use wooden spoon to beat melted chocolate thoroughly into egg yolk and sugar mixture

4 Whisk the egg whites until stiff. Sprinkle in the granulated sugar and continue whisking until glossy to make a light meringue, about 20 seconds.

5 Sift about one-third of the flour over the chocolate mixture, add about one-third of the meringue, and fold together as lightly as possible.

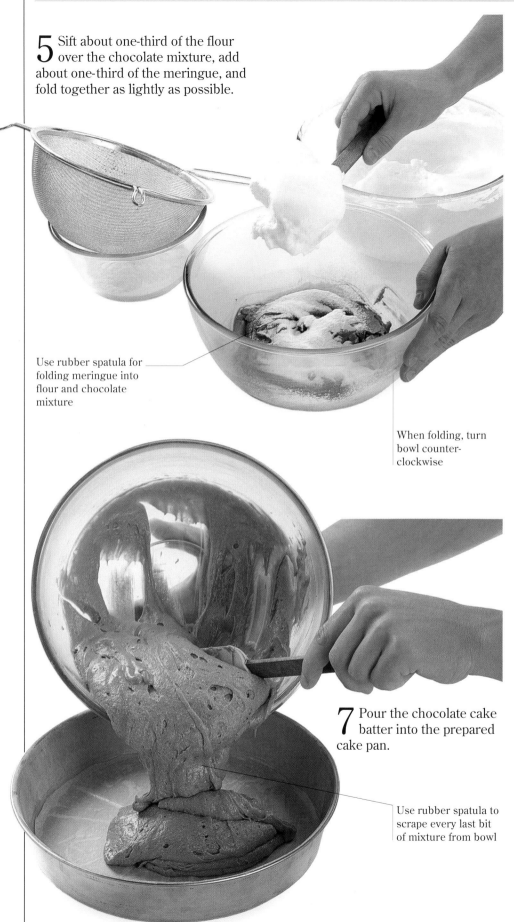

Use rubber spatula for folding meringue into flour and chocolate mixture

When folding, turn bowl counter-clockwise

6 Add the remaining flour and the remaining meringue in the same way, in 2 batches, and fold together as lightly as possible. Cut down into the center of the bowl with the rubber spatula, scoop under the contents and turn them over in a rolling motion.

7 Pour the chocolate cake batter into the prepared cake pan.

Use rubber spatula to scrape every last bit of mixture from bowl

8 Bake in the heated oven until the cake shrinks slightly from the side of the pan and the top springs back when lightly pressed with a finger, 1-1$\frac{1}{4}$ hours. Take the cake from the oven and let cool in the cake pan.

2 MAKE THE APRICOT JAM GLAZE; USE TO COAT THE CAKE

1 With scissors, trim a piece of cardboard into a round slightly smaller than the cake. Make a jam glaze with the apricot jam (see box, right). Run the small knife around the edge of the cooled cake.

2 Set a cardboard round on the cake, then invert the cake onto the wire rack. Set the rack with the tray below to catch the drips from the glaze. Remove the paper.

Invert cake onto rack so cake turns out upside-down on cardboard round and base becomes top

3 Brush top and side of the cake with the warm apricot jam glaze.

HOW TO MAKE JAM GLAZE

Fruit jam glaze is spread on cakes to help keep them moist It can also complement cake flavors.

Melt the jam with the water in a small saucepan. Work it through a strainer into a bowl, return to the pan and melt again over low heat.

Brush glaze evenly over top and side of cake

ANNE SAYS
"Be generous with the glaze because it adds moisture to the cake."

HOW TO MAKE A PAPER PIPING CONE

Disposable paper piping cones are useful for small amounts of icing or filling to be piped with a plain tip, and for those occasions when several colors of icing are being used at once. You can also make a large piping cone and use it in place of a pastry bag, snipping a larger opening in the end and dropping in a piping tube.

Tuck in point
to hold paper
in place

1 Fold an 8- x14-inch rectangle of parchment paper diagonally in half from corner to corner and cut along the fold.

2 Fold the short side of one triangle over to the right-angled corner to form a cone shape.

3 Holding the cone together with one hand, wrap the long point of the triangle around the paper cone with the other hand.

4 Tuck the point of paper inside the cone to secure it. (The remaining triangle of paper can be used for another cone.)

3 MAKE THE CHOCOLATE ICING AND ICE THE CAKE

1 Cut the unsweetened chocolate into large chunks. Chop them with the chef's knife, or in a food processor using the pulse button.

Work melted chocolate from side to side in sweeping motion

2 In a saucepan, heat the sugar, chocolate, and water, stirring until melted. Continue heating to 200°F on the candy thermometer, stirring constantly, then pour onto a marble or laminate surface. Let cool slightly.

3 With the metal spatula, work the mixture vigorously until it cools and thickens to a smooth and shiny consistency, 5-7 minutes.

Pour and spread icing quickly before it sets

Smooth bumps with spatula dipped in hot water

CHOCOLATE RASPBERRY TORTE

Changing the apricot glaze to raspberry gives Sachertorte a surprising twist.

4 When the icing is firm, return it to the saucepan and heat gently until melted and lukewarm. Pour about three-quarters of the icing as quickly as possible on the top of the cake and spread it over the top and side with the metal spatula. Smooth the side, patching gaps with more icing.

! TAKE CARE !
When heating the icing, do not let it get too hot or it will lose its gloss. If necessary to thin it, add a very little water. It must coat a spoon.

ANNE SAYS
"*Use both hands to steady the paper cone while you are piping.*"

1 Prepare and bake the chocolate cake as directed; let cool.
2 Make a jam glaze (see box, page 33), using raspberry jam; use to coat the cake.
3 Ice the cake as directed.
4 If you like, in place of piping the "Sacher" on top, pipe a more simple design, or leave the top of the cake plain if you prefer.
5 Serve with fresh raspberries and whipped cream.

5 Transfer the cake to a serving plate. Make a paper piping cone (see box, page 34). Fill the cone with the remaining icing, using the teaspoon. Fold the top to seal and trim the tip. Pipe "Sacher" on top of the cake.

"Sacher" is perfectly piped with chocolate icing

Chocolate icing is smooth and glossy

BLACK FOREST CAKE

Schwarzwalder Kirschtorte

   SERVES 8-10   WORK TIME 45-50 MINUTES*   BAKING TIME 35-40 MINUTES

EQUIPMENT

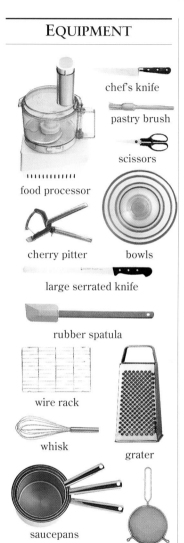

chef's knife

pastry brush

scissors

food processor

cherry pitter   bowls

large serrated knife

rubber spatula

wire rack

grater

whisk

saucepans

strainer

wooden spoon

metal spatula

parchment paper

plate

pastry bag and
medium star tube

8-inch
springform pan   8-10 rose leaves

*Few commercial versions approach the quality of
a Black Forest cake made at home. Rye bread
crumbs are used in the batter, and the cake is
filled with dark cherries and cream.*

* *plus cooling time*

SHOPPING LIST

For the cake batter	
3-4	slices of dark rye bread, total weight about 8 oz
1/3 cup	unsalted butter + extra for pan
1/2 cup	flour + extra for pan
1/2 tsp	baking powder
2 tbsp	cocoa powder
2 oz	semisweet chocolate
3/4 cup	whole blanched almonds
4	eggs
1/2 cup	sugar
1 tbsp	kirsch
1 tbsp	water
For the filling and decoration	
6 oz	semisweet chocolate
1 1/2 cups	dark sweet cherries, fresh or canned in syrup
For the Chantilly cream	
2 cups	heavy cream
2 tbsp	sugar
2 tbsp	kirsch
For the kirsch syrup	
1/3 cup	sugar
1/2 cup	water
2 tbsp	kirsch

INGREDIENTS

dark sweet   semisweet
cherries   chocolate

cocoa powder   kirsch

whole blanched
almonds   dark rye bread

eggs   heavy cream

flour   unsalted butter

baking powder   sugar

ORDER OF WORK

1. **PREPARE AND BAKE THE CAKE**

2. **PREPARE THE FILLING AND DECORATION**

3. **SLICE THE CAKE HORIZONTALLY INTO 3 LAYERS**

4. **ASSEMBLE THE CAKE**

1 PREPARE AND BAKE THE CAKE

1 Heat the oven to 350°F. Butter the cake pan, line the bottom with parchment paper, butter the paper, and flour the pan.

2 Discard the crusts from the bread. Grind the bread to fine crumbs in the food processor or in a blender. Melt the butter and let cool.

Cut slices of bread in half if necessary to fit into feed tube

3 Sift the flour, baking powder, and cocoa powder into a bowl. Cut the chocolate into large chunks. Chop them in the food processor or with the chef's knife. Add to the bowl with the bread crumbs. Stir to mix. Finely grind the almonds in the food processor.

Use large balloon whisk or electric mixer to beat egg yolks and sugar

4 Separate the eggs. In a large bowl, beat the egg yolks with half of the sugar until the mixture is very thick and light in color, about 5 minutes.

5 Add the almonds, kirsch, and water and stir in with the wooden spoon. Set aside.

37

Rubber spatula will scrape all meringue from bowl

6 Whisk the egg whites until stiff. Sprinkle in the remaining sugar and continue whisking until glossy to form a light meringue, about 20 seconds. Add about one-third to the yolk mixture and fold together lightly.

7 Fold the chocolate and bread-crumb mixture into the egg mixture in 3 batches.

8 Fold in the remaining meringue with the rubber spatula.

9 Pour the melted, cooled butter into the chocolate and egg mixture and fold in gently.

10 Pour the batter into the prepared cake pan. Bake the cake in the heated oven until it shrinks slightly from the side of the pan and the top springs back when lightly pressed with a fingertip, 35-40 minutes.

11 Run a knife around the side of the cake to loosen it, then remove the side of the pan. Transfer the cake to the wire rack, placing it upside-down on a piece of parchment paper. Remove the pan base, peel off the lining paper, and let the cake cool. Meanwhile, prepare the filling and decoration.

Parchment paper peels off easily from bottom of cake and does not stick

2 PREPARE THE FILLING AND DECORATION

HOW TO GRATE CHOCOLATE

Grated chocolate makes a simple, attractive garnish for cakes and desserts. It is important that the chocolate be firm, so chill it before grating.

1 Make the chocolate leaves: Melt 3 oz of the chocolate in a bowl set in a saucepan half-filled with hot water; brush the chocolate on the shiny side of each rose leaf in a thin, even layer, leaving a little of the stem exposed. Set the leaves on the plate and let cool, then refrigerate until the chocolate has set. Carefully peel the leaves away from the chocolate.

2 Make the Chantilly cream: Pour the cream into a bowl set in a larger bowl of ice water and whip until soft peaks form. Add the sugar and kirsch and continue whipping until stiff peaks form. Coarsely grate 2 oz of the remaining chocolate (see box, right).

3 For the kirsch syrup, put the sugar into a small saucepan, add the water, and heat until the sugar has dissolved. Bring to a boil and simmer the syrup 1 minute. Remove from the heat and let cool; stir in the kirsch.

If the chocolate is in one large piece, first break it into smaller pieces. When grating, hold the piece of chocolate with a piece of parchment paper or foil to keep it from melting in your hand. Work the chocolate against the largest grid of a grater to obtain coarse chocolate shavings.

4 Reserve 8-10 cherries with stems attached for the decoration. Pit the remaining cherries. If using canned cherries, drain them.

Cherry pitter removes pits neatly

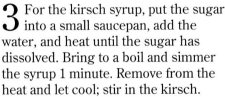

Choose 8-10 perfect cherries with stems attached for decoration

5 Melt the remaining 1 oz chocolate. Dip the cherries with stems into the chocolate to coat evenly. Set the coated cherries on parchment paper and let them cool.

3 Slice the Cake Horizontally into 3 Layers

Vertical cut makes sliced layers easy to line up when reassembling cake so it will be even

Hold hand firmly on top of cake to guide knife

1 If necessary, trim any crusty edges from the cake. With scissors, cut 2 cardboard rounds slightly smaller than the cake; set the cake on top of one round. With the point of the chef's knife, make a small vertical cut in the side of the cake. Using the serrated knife, cut the cake horizontally into 3 even layers.

2 Turn the cake, not the knife, as you cut the layers with an even, broad slicing motion.

4 Assemble the Cake

Use metal spatula to spread cream gently over cherries

1 Brush the cooled kirsch syrup evenly on each of the cake layers to moisten.

2 Spread the bottom cake layer with one-eighth of the Chantilly cream. Top with half of the pitted cherries. Spread with another one-eighth cream.

3 Lift the middle cake layer with the second cardboard round, set it on the bottom layer, and press down lightly. Brush with more kirsch syrup.

Slide cardboard round from under cake layer as it is set over cream and cherries

4 Fill the second layer in the same way as the first, using another one-quarter of the remaining Chantilly cream and the remaining cherries.

5 Set the top cake layer in place, cut-side down. Transfer the cake on the cardboard round to a bowl or cake stand.

With fingers, gently press top cake layer into cream so it will sit firmly on cake

6 Neaten the side of the cake by smoothing any cream that has pressed out between the layers.

7 Spread half of the remaining Chantilly cream smoothly over the top and side of the cake.

8 Press the grated chocolate around the side, using a piece of parchment paper to help.

Plate underneath cake catches grated chocolate as it falls

9 Transfer the cake to a serving plate. Mark a lattice on top of the cake with the edge of the metal spatula.

Hold metal spatula at right angles to cake

Gently press edge of spatula into cream to make thin grooves

10 Put the remaining Chantilly cream into the pastry bag with the medium star tube and pipe rosettes around the top edge of the cake.

When piping rosettes, hold pastry bag upright and squeeze gently

🍴 **TO SERVE**
Top the rosettes with the chocolate-dipped cherries and add the chocolate leaves.

Cherry and Chantilly cream filling is revealed when cake is sliced

VARIATION
BLACK FOREST STRIP CAKE

1 Prepare the cake batter as directed in the main recipe.
2 In place of the springform cake pan, butter a large baking sheet, line it with parchment paper, and butter the paper. Spread the batter on the baking sheet in a 12- x 15-inch rectangle.
3 Bake the cake until the top springs back when pressed with a fingertip, 7-10 minutes.
4 Trim the crusty edges from the cake and cut it lengthwise into 3 equal strips.
5 Fill and layer the cake strips as directed.
6 To decorate, pipe the remaining Chantilly cream on top using a plain tube and sprinkle lightly with grated chocolate. Omit the chocolate leaves and chocolate-coated cherries if you like.

GETTING AHEAD
The cake can be baked 3 days ahead and stored in an airtight container. After filling, it can be kept, covered, in the refrigerator 12-24 hours and the flavors will mellow. The chocolate leaves can be layered with parchment paper and stored in the refrigerator up to 1 week. Assemble the cake not more than 2 hours before serving.

HOW TO MAKE AND CRUSH PRALINE

Praline is made by caramelizing equal weights of sugar and whole unblanched almonds directly over low heat. The nuts should be thoroughly toasted to develop their flavor. Praline can be kept several weeks in an airtight container at room temperature. It can also be frozen.

1 Lightly brush a baking sheet or marble slab with oil. Combine the nuts and sugar in a heavy-based saucepan. Heat gently until the sugar melts, stirring often with a wooden spoon. Continue cooking over fairly low heat to a medium caramel, stirring lightly. The sugar should be a deep golden brown and the almonds should make a popping sound, showing that they are toasted.

2 Remove the pan from the heat and immediately pour the sugar mixture onto the oiled baking sheet or marble slab. Spread out the praline with the wooden spoon and leave it until cool and crisp, 10-15 minutes.

! TAKE CARE !
The mixture is very hot when pouring it from the pan onto the baking sheet.

3 To crush the praline: Crack the praline into pieces with a rolling pin, then grind to the desired consistency in a food processor or blender. For a more even texture, grind the praline in 3 or 4 batches.

ANNE SAYS
"For large chunks of praline, put the praline in a thick plastic bag and pound it into pieces with a rolling pin."

CHOCOLATE PRALINE CAKE

Crunchy praline made with toasted almonds and caramel replaces the cherries in Black Forest Cake. Use rum for flavoring the syrup instead of kirsch. The cake is best served the day it is made.

1 Prepare and bake the cake as directed.
2 Make praline (see box, left), using 1¼ cups whole unblanched almonds and ¾ cup sugar, and separating 8-10 whole caramel-coated almonds for the garnish. When the sheet of praline has set, crush it finely.
3 Make the Chantilly cream.
4 Mix two-thirds of the finely crushed praline into two-thirds of the Chantilly cream. Use the cream for filling, reserving enough to decorate the top.
5 Assemble the cake as directed, omitting the cherries and grated chocolate.
6 Cover the top and side of the cake with the plain Chantilly cream. Omit the lattice.
7 Press the remaining praline around the side and pipe rosettes of the reserved praline Chantilly cream in a ring on top of the cake.
8 Garnish with the caramel-coated almonds.

CHOCOLATE CHESTNUT ROLL

 SERVES 8-10   WORK TIME 50-55 MINUTES   BAKING TIME 5-7 MINUTES

EQUIPMENT

 whisk*

 chef's knife

bowls

serrated knife

 saucepans

plain dish towel or large napkin   pastry bag and small star tube

 rose leaves   metal spatula

parchment paper

wooden spoon   strainer

 chopping board   plate

pastry brush

baking sheets

 rubber spatula
*electric mixer can also be used

A winter favorite, especially for the holiday season, this rolled sponge cake is filled with a rich chestnut purée mixed with whipped cream. Decorated with piped cream, candied chestnuts, and delicate chocolate leaves, it looks superb.

GETTING AHEAD

Once the cake is assembled, it will keep 1-2 days in the refrigerator. Add the cream decoration, candied chestnuts and chocolate leaves just before serving.

SHOPPING LIST

	For the chocolate sponge roll
	butter for baking sheet
5 tbsp	cocoa powder
1 tbsp	flour
	salt
5	eggs
³⁄₄ cup	sugar
	For the filling
³⁄₄ cup	heavy cream
4 oz	chestnut purée
2 tbsp	dark rum
1 oz	semisweet chocolate
	sugar to taste (optional)
	To finish and decorate
3 oz	semisweet chocolate for chocolate leaves
¹⁄₄ cup	sugar
¹⁄₄ cup	water
2 tbsp	dark rum
¹⁄₂ cup	heavy cream
8-10	candied chestnuts

INGREDIENTS

 eggs   heavy cream

 flour

 chestnut purée   candied chestnuts

 cocoa powder

 semisweet chocolate   dark rum

 sugar

ORDER OF WORK

1 MAKE THE CHOCOLATE BATTER

2 BAKE, UNMOLD, AND ROLL THE SPONGE

3 MAKE THE FILLING

4 FINISH AND DECORATE THE CAKE

1 MAKE THE CHOCOLATE BATTER

1 Heat the oven to 425° F. Brush a 12- x 15-inch baking sheet with melted butter, line with parchment paper, and butter the paper.

Be sure to cover entire surface of baking sheet

Melted butter is easy to brush on evenly

2 Sift the cocoa powder, flour, and a pinch of salt into a bowl.

Color of egg yolk mixture will lighten as you whisk

3 Separate the eggs. Beat the egg yolks with two-thirds of the sugar until light, and the mixture leaves a ribbon trail when the whisk is lifted, about 3-5 minutes.

4 Whisk the egg whites until stiff. Sprinkle in the remaining sugar and continue whisking until glossy to make a light meringue, about 20 seconds.

ANNE SAYS
"Your bowl and whisk must be completely free of any trace of water, grease, or egg yolk or the egg whites will not whisk to full volume."

When folding, cut down through mixture and move spatula down and around; turn bowl counter-clockwise with other hand

5 Sift about one-third of the cocoa mixture over the egg-yolk mixture.

ANNE SAYS
"Double sifting ensures the cocoa powder will be evenly distributed."

6 Add one-third of the meringue. Fold the mixtures together as lightly as possible. Add the remaining cocoa mixture and meringue in the same way in 2 batches.

2 BAKE, UNMOLD, AND ROLL THE SPONGE

1 Pour the chocolate batter, all at once, onto the prepared baking sheet. Use the rubber spatula to scrape out the bowl.

2 Spread the batter evenly on the baking sheet almost to the edges. Put in the heated oven, near the bottom, and bake about 5-7 minutes. The cake is done when it is risen and just firm to the touch. Do not overbake the cake or it will be difficult to roll.

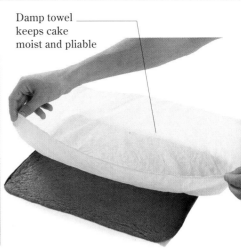

Damp towel keeps cake moist and pliable

3 Dampen the dish towel. Remove the cake from the oven and immediately cover with the dish towel.

Put second baking sheet on top of damp towel so cake can be turned over easily

4 Take a second baking sheet and set it on top of the cake. Quickly invert the cake so the original baking sheet is on top. Place the cake on the work surface and carefully remove the uppermost baking sheet.

5 Holding the parchment paper by its edges, peel it off the cake.

6 Starting at the short end nearest you, fold over the end of the towel so it overlaps the cake and then tightly roll up the cake lengthwise. Set aside to cool.

Using even pressure, roll down length from short end

3 MAKE THE FILLING

Rubber spatula is ideal for folding mixtures

1 Pour the cream into a chilled bowl and whip until it forms soft peaks and just holds a shape.

ANNE SAYS
"Set the chilled bowl in a larger one filled with ice water. This helps keep cream chilled, and is especially effective in hot weather."

2 Put the chestnut purée in another bowl and add the rum; this will soften the purée. Cut the chocolate into large chunks, then chop with the chef's knife, or in a food processor. Melt the chocolate in a bowl set in a saucepan half-filled with hot water. Add to the chestnut purée and stir well with the wooden spoon to remove any lumps.

3 Stir about 2 tbsp of the whipped cream into the mixture to soften it, then fold the chocolate-chestnut mixture into the rest of the whipped cream. If necessary, add sugar to taste.

4 FINISH AND DECORATE THE CAKE

Carefully unroll cooled cake

1 Use the 3 oz semisweet chocolate to make 8-10 chocolate leaves (see box, page 48). Reserve for the decoration.

2 Make a rum syrup: In a small saucepan, over low heat, heat half of the sugar in the water until it dissolves. Simmer the syrup 1 minute. Let cool, then stir in the rum.

3 Unroll the cake, then roll it up again without the towel. Place the cake on a sheet of parchment paper and unroll it. The smooth top will be on the outside when rolled.

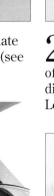

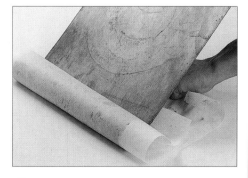

4 Brush the top of the cake with the cooled rum syrup. Using the metal spatula, spread the chestnut filling evenly over the top.

5 Using the paper underneath, carefully roll up the filled cake as tightly as possible.

6 Bring the paper up over the cake; fold it in tightly. Insert the edge of the baking sheet against the fold and push away from you to tighten the roll.

HOW TO MAKE CHOCOLATE LEAVES

If melted chocolate is brushed on leaves and left to set, the original leaves can be peeled off, leaving chocolate facsimiles. Pliable leaves with deep veins, such as rose and ficus, are best. Chocolate leaves can be layered with parchment paper and then stored in the refrigerator up to 1 week.

1 Cut the chocolate into large chunks. Chop them with a chef's knife, or in a food processor using the pulse button. Melt the chocolate in a bowl set in a saucepan half-filled with hot water. For a shiny finish on the leaves, temper the chocolate (see page 55). Using a pastry brush or your fingertip, spread chocolate on the shiny side of each leaf in a thin even layer, leaving a little of the stem exposed so it is easy to peel off the leaf. Set the leaves on a plate and let cool; refrigerate until set.

2 With the tips of your fingers, peel the leaves away from the chocolate, handling as little as possible so it does not melt and become dull.

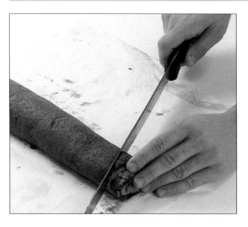

7 With the serrated knife, cut each end of the cake on the diagonal. Transfer the cake to a serving plate for decorating.

8 Pour the cream into a chilled bowl and whip until soft peaks form. Add the remaining sugar and continue whipping until stiff peaks form and the whisk leaves clear marks. Fill the pastry bag with the cream.

9 Pipe a continuous wavy line of whipped cream over the rolled cake. Arrange the chocolate leaves and candied chestnuts along each side of the roll.

Hold pastry bag steady so waves of cream are even

Piped whipped cream adds interest to plain top of rolled cake

Candied chestnuts (*marrons glacés*) alternate with chocolate leaves

VARIATION
CHOCOLATE STRAWBERRY CREAM CAKE

This cake has a lighter filling than that in the main recipe. With its strawberry sauce, it is ideal for summer occasions.

1 Make and roll up the chocolate sponge as directed.
2 Whip ¾ cup heavy cream with 2 tbsp sugar. Fold 1 cup chopped strawberries into the cream.
3 Make the sugar syrup, using kirsch instead of rum, and brush over the cake.
4 Fill and roll up the cake as directed.
5 Dip fresh strawberries in melted chocolate and leave to set on parchment paper.

6 Meanwhile, make a strawberry coulis: Hull 1 quart strawberries, washing them only if dirty. Purée the strawberries in a food processor. Stir in 2 tbsp kirsch (optional), and 2-3 tbsp confectioners' sugar to taste.
7 Slice the cake and arrange on individual plates with pools of strawberry coulis. Decorate with chocolate-dipped strawberries.

VARIATION
CHOCOLATE NUT CREAM CAKE WITH CARAMEL SAUCE

This version has a filling of crunchy praline and a creamy caramel sauce.

1 Make and roll up the chocolate sponge as directed.
2 Make praline: Lightly brush a baking sheet or marble slab with oil. Heat ¾ cup unblanched hazelnuts and ½ cup sugar in a heavy-based saucepan until the sugar melts, stirring often with a wooden spoon. Continue cooking over fairly low heat to a medium caramel, stirring lightly. The sugar should be a deep golden brown and the hazelnuts should make a popping sound.
3 Immediately pour the mixture onto the oiled baking sheet or marble slab. Spread out the praline with the wooden spoon and leave until cool and crisp, 10-15 minutes.
4 Reserve some whole hazelnuts coated with caramel for decoration. Crack the remainder into pieces with a rolling pin, then coarsely grind in a food processor or blender.
5 Whip ¾ cup heavy cream as directed. Fold in the ground praline.
6 Omit the rum syrup. Spread two-thirds of the hazelnut-praline cream on the chocolate sponge, then roll up, and trim as directed.
7 Make the caramel cream sauce (see box, right). Drizzle some sauce on individual plates. Set 2 cake slices on each plate. Serve with additional sauce.

HOW TO MAKE CARAMEL CREAM SAUCE

A caramel cream sauce has so many uses – with cake, over ice cream, or with a fruit pie.

1 Gently heat 1 cup sugar and ½ cup water in a heavy-based saucepan until the sugar is dissolved. Boil without stirring until the syrup starts to turn golden around the edge. Reduce the heat and continue cooking until the caramel is deep golden in color.

ANNE SAYS
"Let the caramel cook to a deep golden or it will be tasteless, but do not overcook – it burns easily."

2 Remove the caramel from the heat and immediately pour in ¾ cup hot heavy cream. Whisk immediately to mix, then let cool.

! TAKE CARE !
The caramel may splutter when the cream is added, so stand at arm's length when pouring.

CHECKERBOARD CAKE WITH CHOCOLATE GANACHE

🍽 SERVES 8-10 🥄 WORK TIME 50-55 MINUTES* 🍲 BAKING TIME 15-20 MINUTES

EQUIPMENT

electric mixer

scissors

chef's knife

metal spatulas

rubber spatula

saucepans

wooden spoon

ladle   bowl strainers

whisk

pastry brush   conical strainer

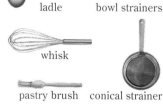

3 8-inch round cake pans   3 pastry bags

parchment paper

bowls

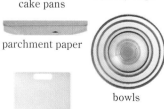

chopping board

metal skewer

The checkerboard in this tall cake is hidden by a rich chocolate ganache frosting wrapped with a chocolate ribbon. Only when cut is the checkered chocolate and vanilla interior of the cake revealed.

plus cooling and chilling time

INGREDIENTS

semisweet chocolate

confectioners' sugar

heavy cream

kirsch

eggs

cocoa powder

vanilla extract

unsalted butter

granulated sugar

raspberry jam

flour

baking powder

SHOPPING LIST

For the cake	
1 cup	unsalted butter + extra for pan
3 cups	flour
1½ tbsp	baking powder
⅓ cup	cocoa powder
2¼ cups	confectioners' sugar
6	eggs
2 tsp	vanilla extract
4 oz	semisweet chocolate for the ribbon
2 tbsp	cocoa powder for dusting
For the kirsch syrup	
½ cup	water
½ cup	granulated sugar
2-3 tbsp	kirsch
For the raspberry jam glaze	
⅓ cup	raspberry jam
2-3 tbsp	water
For the chocolate ganache	
8 oz	semisweet chocolate
1 cup	heavy cream

ORDER OF WORK

1 MAKE THE CAKE BATTERS

2 PREPARE THE CHECKERBOARD PATTERN AND BAKE THE CAKE

3 ASSEMBLE THE CHECKERBOARD

4 DECORATE THE CAKE

1 MAKE THE CAKE BATTERS

1 Heat the oven to 375°F. Butter the cake pans and line the bottom of each with parchment paper. Butter the paper.

Parchment paper sticks to melted butter brushed on bottom of pan

Circle of parchment paper has been cut from folded square so it fits exactly inside pan

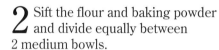

2 Sift the flour and baking powder and divide equally between 2 medium bowls.

Tap side of strainer to help sugar go through

Confectioners' sugar will cream more easily with butter if it is sifted

3 Sift the cocoa powder into one of the bowls, tapping the side of the strainer to remove any lumps. Beat the butter in a large bowl with the wooden spoon or electric mixer until creamy.

4 Sift the confectioners' sugar into the butter and beat in thoroughly.

5 Continue beating the butter and sugar mixture with the wooden spoon or mixer until the mixture is light and fluffy, 2-3 minutes.

6 Add the eggs one by one, stirring well after each addition. Add the vanilla extract and stir into the creamed mixture until evenly blended.

ANNE SAYS
"If the mixture begins to separate when adding the eggs, heat the bowl gently over hot water."

Cake batters that are rich in eggs, as this one is, may separate and have curdled appearance

After heating bowl gently over hot water, curdled cake batter will become creamy again

7 Divide the cake batter in half and add the cocoa and flour mixture to one portion. Stir well to mix. Stir the plain flour mixture into the other.

2 PREPARE THE CHECKERBOARD PATTERN AND BAKE THE CAKE

1 Fit 2 of the pastry bags with ½-inch plain tubes. Fill 1 bag with cocoa batter, and the other with white batter (see box, page 53). Pipe a ring of chocolate batter against the sides of 2 of the cake pans.

ANNE SAYS
"If your pastry bags are small, you may need to fill them in 2 batches."

Pipe 2 rings of chocolate and 2 of white batter in each pan, alternating colors, then fill in center

2 Pipe a ring of white batter against the side of the third cake pan. Pipe a ring of the white batter inside the chocolate rings in the first 2 cake pans. Continue alternating rings of chocolate and white batter until all of the cake pans are full.

3 Bake the layers until the cakes start to shrink from the sides of the pans and the skewer inserted in the centers comes out clean, 15-20 minutes. Meanwhile, make the syrup and glaze (see page 53).

3 ASSEMBLE THE CHECKERBOARD

1 Make the kirsch syrup: Heat the water and sugar in a small pan until the sugar has dissolved. Simmer the syrup 1 minute, remove from the heat, and let cool. Stir in the kirsch.

2 Make the raspberry jam glaze: In another small saucepan, heat the raspberry jam and water, stirring until the jam has melted.

3 Pour the raspberry jam glaze through the conical strainer into a bowl; return the glaze to the saucepan. With kitchen scissors, trim a piece of cardboard into a round slightly smaller than the cake.

HOW TO FILL A PASTRY BAG

A variety of tubes can be used with a pastry bag: Plain tubes are suitable for piping cake batters and shaping meringue, while fluted tubes are used for whipped cream decorations.

1 Drop the tube into the pastry bag. Twist the bag, tucking the bag into the tube with your finger.

ANNE SAYS
"Twisting and tucking keeps filling from leaking out at the bottom."

Moisten cake layers with kirsch syrup

2 Fold the top of the bag over your hand to form a collar and add the mixture to be piped, scraping the rubber spatula against the bag.

3 When the pastry bag is full, unfold the top and twist the top until there is no air left in it.

4 Remove the cake layers from the oven. Brush the kirsch syrup on each layer of cake while the layers are still hot.

5 Unmold the cakes onto a wire rack and peel off the paper.

Melt strained raspberry jam glaze over low heat before brushing over cake so it will spread easily

6 Brush the base of each layer with the remaining syrup. Place the cardboard round under one of the cake layers with an outer chocolate ring. Reheat the jam glaze, and brush half of it on the cake layer.

Brush jam glaze evenly all over top of cake and right up to edge

7 Top with the cake that has the outer plain ring and brush it with the remaining jam glaze. Place the remaining cake with the outer chocolate ring on top of the middle layer. Let the cake cool while making the ganache.

4 DECORATE THE CAKE

1 Make the chocolate ganache: Cut the chocolate into large chunks. Chop them with the chef's knife, or in a food processor using the pulse button. Put the chocolate in a medium bowl. Bring the cream to a boil in a small saucepan and pour it over the chopped chocolate.

2 Whisk the chopped chocolate and cream together until the chocolate has melted completely.

3 Continue beating, with the electric mixer or the whisk, until the ganache is fluffy and cool, 5-10 minutes.

! TAKE CARE !
Do not overbeat the mixture or it will be very stiff and hard to spread.

HOW TO TEMPER MELTED CHOCOLATE

Tempering makes melted chocolate more malleable and shiny. Covering chocolate (couverture) is most often tempered because it has a high cocoa butter content with the greatest gloss. This method is classic, ideal for large amounts of chocolate, while the quicker method, right, is best for smaller amounts.

Make sure work surface is completely dry before pouring melted chocolate onto it

How to temper chocolate quickly
This method is easier than the classic method, left, and can be used for smaller amounts. After melting chocolate, stir it gently until it reaches 115°F on a candy thermometer and is very smooth.

Set the bowl of melted chocolate in a bowl of cool (not ice) water. Stir often until it cools to 80°F, 3-5 minutes, then set it in the pan of hot water and heat it to 90°F.

1 Stir melted chocolate gently until it reaches 115°F on a candy thermometer and is very smooth.

2 Pour two-thirds of the chocolate onto a smooth work surface, such as marble or laminate.

3 Work the chocolate by spreading it back and forth with a metal spatula for at least 3 minutes until it is thick and on the point of setting (about 80°F).

4 Using 2 metal spatulas, quickly transfer the chocolate from the marble to the reserved chocolate in the bowl. Reheat it in the saucepan of hot water, stirring constantly, to 90°F.

4 Reserve one-third of the ganache frosting for piping on top of the cake. Using a metal spatula, spread the side of the cake with some of the remaining ganache frosting.

5 Spread the remainder on top of the cake with the metal spatula, and fill in any gaps between the layers – the side should be straight and even.

Warm spatula first so it will spread frosting smoothly

6 Make the chocolate ribbon: Cut a 4- x 24-inch strip from a sheet of parchment paper (it should be the same height as the cake).

7 Chop the chocolate and melt it in a bowl set in a saucepan half-filled with hot water. For a shiny finish on the chocolate ribbon, temper the melted chocolate (see box, page 55).

Spread chocolate gently with even pressure

8 Ladle the cooled melted or tempered chocolate onto the parchment strip. With a metal spatula, quickly spread the chocolate in an even layer about 1/16-inch thick.

9 Immediately wrap the chocolate ribbon around the cake, paper-side out.

Wrap ribbon around cake while chocolate is still soft; it will then set onto side of cake

10 If the paper overlaps, cut it with scissors.

11 Fit the remaining pastry bag with a 3/8-inch plain tube. Put in the remaining ganache (see box, page 53) and pipe it in "tear-drop" shapes on top of the cake, starting at the edge and working toward the center.

ANNE SAYS
"*Slightly overlap tear-drop shapes and pipe them in concentric circles to cover top of cake completely.*"

Pipe ganache in tear-drop shapes

12 Sift the cocoa powder over the top of the cake. Refrigerate until the chocolate ribbon is set, about 1 hour.

If any lumps of cocoa powder are left in bottom of strainer, work them through with your fingertips

13 Carefully peel the parchment paper from the chocolate ribbon round the cake.

🍽 TO SERVE

Carefully transfer the cake from its cardboard round to a serving plate. Keep the cake in the refrigerator until serving time.

GETTING AHEAD
The cake can be kept in the refrigerator up to 2 days.

Chocolate ribbon is wrapped around cake

APRICOT CHECKERBOARD CAKE

1 Make the cake batters and pipe into the prepared round pans as directed.
2 Bake the layers and brush with syrup as directed.
3 Make the glaze with apricot rather than raspberry jam and brush it over the layers.
4 Make the chocolate ganache and frost the cake.
5 Omit the chocolate ribbon and make an apricot sauce: Drain 10 oz canned apricots in syrup and set aside 4 apricot halves for the decoration; reserve the syrup. Purée the remaining apricots in a food processor or blender, then work through a strainer. Add a little of the reserved syrup to make a sauce of pourable consistency, then stir in 1-2 tbsp kirsch if desired.
6 Arrange slices of cake on individual plates; spoon the apricot sauce around. Decorate with apricot slices.

Checkerboard pattern is revealed when cake is sliced

CHOCOLATE CREME BRULEE

Crème Brûlée au Chocolat

🍽 SERVES 4   🥄 WORK TIME 15-20 MINUTES*   ♨ BAKING TIME 10-15 MINUTES

EQUIPMENT

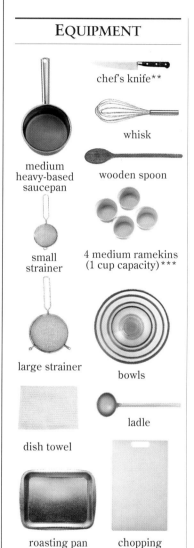

chef's knife**

whisk

medium heavy-based saucepan

wooden spoon

small strainer

4 medium ramekins (1 cup capacity)***

large strainer

bowls

ladle

dish towel

roasting pan

chopping board

**food processor can also be used
***gratin dishes can also be used

This classic cream is flavored with dark chocolate, lightly set with egg yolks, and topped with a thin layer of caramelized sugar. You can use ramekins for baking the cream, or individual gratin dishes if you want the maximum area of crisp caramel topping. Instead of broiling, professional chefs use a portable blow torch for caramelizing the cream without overcooking it. The flame is held several inches from the cream and the sugar is heated until bubbling and brown. Using this method, there is no need to put the cream in the roasting pan with the ice, because the flame is directed only at the sugar and does not heat the cream.

GETTING AHEAD

The chocolate creams can be made up to 8 hours ahead and kept refrigerated. Caramelize the sugar not more than 2 hours before serving.

* plus 1-8 hours chilling time

SHOPPING LIST

6 oz	semisweet chocolate
2 cups	heavy cream
4	egg yolks
1/4 cup	sugar for sprinkling

INGREDIENTS

semisweet chocolate

heavy cream

egg yolks

sugar

ANNE SAYS

"With so few ingredients, the key to a good crème brûlée is that each should be of highest quality. Most important is good-quality chocolate, which makes all the difference. Also important is the cream used – standard heavy cream, with a fat content of about 40%, adds richness and smoothness, and should be used rather than whipping or light cream with lower fat contents."

ORDER OF WORK

1 MAKE THE CHOCOLATE CREAMS

2 CARAMELIZE THE CHOCOLATE CREAMS

HOW TO CHOP CHOCOLATE

Chill chocolate on a warm day before chopping. Chopping board must be dry, because moisture can affect melting.

1 On a chopping board, with a chef's knife, cut chocolate into small chunks.

2 **To chop by hand:** With broad end of knife, chop until chocolate is fine. Rock handle up and down, holding tip down with heel of other hand.

To chop in a food processor: Put chocolate chunks into food processor, then chop using the pulse button. If necessary, chop chocolate in several batches.

! TAKE CARE !
Do not overwork the chocolate or the heat of the machine may melt it.

1 MAKE THE CHOCOLATE CREAMS

1 Heat the oven to 400° F. Chop the chocolate (see box, left). Heat the chocolate with the cream in the saucepan, stirring with the wooden spoon, until melted and smooth. Bring just to a boil. Let cool slightly.

Add chopped chocolate to cream and melt in heavy-based pan to prevent mixture burning

2 Put the egg yolks in a large bowl and whisk together until just mixed.

Whisk gently so mixture does not become frothy

3 Pour the chocolate cream slowly into the egg yolks, whisking constantly until evenly mixed.

4 Strain the chocolate cream through the large strainer to remove any bits of cooked egg yolk.

Rest bowl strainer on rim of bowl

Strain chocolate cream to remove any bits of egg

5 Carefully ladle the chocolate cream into the ramekins, dividing it equally among them.

6 Fold the dish towel and put on the bottom of the roasting pan; set the ramekins on the towel. Pour in cold water to come just over halfway up the sides of the dishes.

Towel protects chocolate creams from direct heat of roasting pan and prevents water from bubbling up into them

7 Bake the chocolate creams in the oven until a thin skin forms on top, 10-15 minutes. Remove the ramekins from the roasting pan. Chill the chocolate creams in the refrigerator at least 1 hour or up to 8 hours.

ANNE SAYS
"The chocolate cream underneath the skin will still be soft."

2 CARAMELIZE THE CHOCOLATE CREAMS

1 Heat the broiler. Sprinkle each chocolate cream evenly with sugar, using the small strainer, to form a thin even layer.

! TAKE CARE !
Wipe off any sugar from the edges of the dishes because it will burn under the broiler.

Ice water ensures chocolate cream does not heat under broiler

2 Half fill the roasting pan with cold water and ice, and set the ramekins in it. Broil the chocolate creams as close as possible to the heat until the sugar melts and caramelizes, 2-3 minutes. Let cool a few minutes so the caramel forms a crisp layer.

ANNE SAYS
"*It is essential that the sugar is broiled under very high heat so it caramelizes before the cream overcooks.*"

TO SERVE
Place each ramekin on an individual plate. Crack the caramel with the back of a spoon to arrive at the chocolate cream beneath.

Thin, crisp caramel layer is cracked to reveal rich chocolate cream underneath

VARIATION

CHOCOLATE CREME BRULEE WITH RASPBERRIES

Fresh raspberries are a delicious surprise hidden in the bottom of each chocolate cream.

1 Make the chocolate cream mixture as directed.
2 Sprinkle 2-3 tbsp fresh raspberries in the bottom of each of 4 gratin dishes, then fill the dishes with the chocolate cream.
3 Bake the creams and caramelize the sugar as directed.
4 Decorate each cream with a few raspberries just before serving.

CHOCOLATE ORANGE TRUFFLE CAKE

🍽 SERVES 10-12   🥄 WORK TIME 35-40 MINUTES*   🍲 BAKING TIME ABOUT 40 MINUTES

EQUIPMENT

- 10-inch round cake pan
- electric mixer**
- chef's knife
- 9-inch springform pan
- small knife
- vegetable peeler
- kitchen scissors
- pastry brush
- bowls
- strainers
- plastic wrap
- saucepans
- wire rack
- chopping board
- parchment paper
- metal spatula
- rubber spatula

**whisk can also be used

A layer of chocolate sponge cake is crowned with chocolate ganache flavored with Grand Marnier. Sifted cocoa and a cluster of white chocolate curls complete the ultimate chocolate indulgence. Orange sections steeped in orange juice and Grand Marnier provide the perfect complement.

* *plus at least 6 hours chilling time*

SHOPPING LIST

For the cake layer	
	butter and flour for pans
¼ cup	butter
¾ cup	flour
¼ cup	cocoa powder
	salt
4	eggs
⅔ cup	sugar
4-5 tbsp	Grand Marnier
For the chocolate ganache	
12 oz	semisweet chocolate
1½ cups	heavy cream
3 tbsp	Grand Marnier
To decorate and finish	
1	bar white chocolate for curls
6	oranges
3 tbsp	Grand Marnier
3 tbsp	cocoa powder

INGREDIENTS

- semisweet chocolate
- white chocolate
- flour
- eggs
- heavy cream
- butter
- sugar
- oranges
- Grand Marnier
- cocoa powder

ORDER OF WORK

1. **MAKE THE CAKE LAYER**

2. **PREPARE THE BASE**

3. **MAKE THE CHOCOLATE GANACHE**

4. **PREPARE THE DECORATION AND FINISH THE CAKE**

MAKE THE CAKE LAYER

1 Heat the oven to 425° F. Butter the cake pan and line the bottom with parchment paper. Butter the paper.

2 Sprinkle in 2-3 tbsp flour and turn the pan to coat the bottom and side evenly; tap the pan upside down to remove excess flour. Melt the butter and let it cool.

Coat cake pan lightly and evenly with flour

3 Sift together the flour, cocoa powder, and a pinch of salt.

Mixture will become pale and thick

4 Put the eggs in a large bowl and beat with the electric mixer for a few seconds to mix. Add the sugar to the eggs and continue beating at high speed until the mixture leaves a ribbon trail when the beaters are lifted, about 5 minutes.

Lift beaters above mixture from time to time to see if it is thick enough to leave a ribbon trail

ANNE SAYS

"*If using a whisk, set the mixture over a pan of hot but not boiling water and whisk vigorously by hand, about 10 minutes.*"

5 Sift about one-third of the flour and cocoa mixture over the egg mixture and fold the mixtures together as lightly as possible. Add another third of the flour and cocoa mixture and fold together in the same way.

Fold very lightly with rubber spatula

Folded dish towel underneath bowl will keep it steady as you add melted butter

6 Add the remaining flour and cocoa mixture and the cooled, melted butter and fold them in gently but quickly.

7 Pour the mixture into the prepared cake pan, then tap the pan on the work surface to level the mixture and knock out air bubbles.

8 Bake in the heated oven until the cake is risen and just firm to the touch, about 40 minutes. Turn the cake out onto the wire rack. Peel off the paper. Let the cake cool.

2 PREPARE THE BASE

1 Trim the cooled cake to fit the springform pan, using the base of the pan as a guide.

Hold small knife vertically and cut cake around base of springform pan with up-and-down sawing action

2 Lightly butter the bottom and side of the springform pan. Carefully transfer the trimmed cake to the pan. Sprinkle the 4-5 tbsp Grand Marnier over the top of the cake. Cover and set aside while making the chocolate ganache.

3 MAKE THE CHOCOLATE GANACHE

Hot cream will melt chocolate

1 Cut the chocolate into large chunks. Chop them with the chef's knife or in a food processor. Put the chocolate in a large bowl.

2 Heat the cream until almost boiling, then pour it over the chopped chocolate. Stir until the chocolate has melted. Let cool, stirring occasionally.

3 Add the 3 tbsp Grand Marnier to the cream and chocolate mixture, and stir until blended.

4 Using the electric mixer, beat the chocolate ganache until fluffy, 5-10 minutes.

! TAKE CARE !
Do not overbeat the mixture or it will be very stiff and hard to spread.

5 With the rubber spatula, or a wooden spoon, transfer the chocolate ganache to the top of the cake and smooth the surface. Cover with plastic wrap and chill until firm, at least 6 hours.

4 PREPARE THE DECORATION AND FINISH THE CAKE

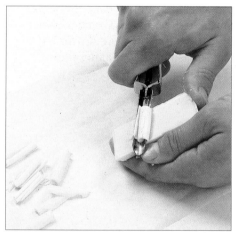

1 Using the vegetable peeler, shave curls from the white chocolate bar onto parchment paper or a plate.

2 Trim both ends of each orange, set the fruit upright on the chopping board, and cut away the peel and all pith, following the curve of the fruit.

3 Working over a bowl, cut down each side of the orange sections to separate them from the membranes. Put the sections in the bowl; sprinkle over the Grand Marnier.

Cut off peel, working from top to bottom

4 Just before serving, take the cake from the refrigerator. Stand it on top of a bowl, then remove the side of the pan.

5 Mask the center of the cake with a 3-inch round of parchment paper. Sift the cocoa powder on top of the cake and carefully remove the paper round.

Parchment paper round keeps center of cake plain for white chocolate curls

6 Transfer the cake to a serving plate, using the metal spatula, and sprinkle the white chocolate curls over the center of the cake. Sift a little cocoa powder over the white chocolate curls.

White chocolate curls are decorative contrast

TO SERVE Slice the cake neatly, then place on individual plates. Arrange orange sections next to the cake and spoon a little of the orange liquid over them.

V A R I A T I O N
CHOCOLATE-COFFEE TRUFFLE CAKE

Here coffee-flavored liqueur replaces the Grand Marnier in Chocolate Orange Truffle Cake.

1 Prepare and bake the chocolate sponge cake, trim the cake to fit the springform pan, and sprinkle over 4-5 tbsp Tia Maria or other coffee-flavored liqueur.

2 Make the ganache, replacing the Grand Marnier with Tia Maria. Spread the ganache over the cake. Chill as directed.

3 Omit the chocolate curls and orange sections and decorate the top of the cake with 3 oz chocolate coffee beans, pressing them lightly onto the surface. Sift cocoa powder over the top, then decorate with a few more chocolate coffee beans.

—— GETTING AHEAD ——
The chocolate sponge cake and ganache can be made and layered 1 day in advance and kept, covered, in the refrigerator. The curls can also be made 1 day in advance. Unmold and decorate the cake 1-2 hours before serving.

CHOCOLATE CHARLOTTE

 SERVES 6-8 WORK TIME 40-45 MINUTES* BAKING TIME 45-55 MINUTES

EQUIPMENT

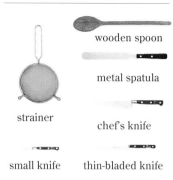

wooden spoon

metal spatula

strainer

chef's knife

small knife   thin-bladed knife

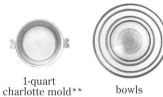

1-quart
charlotte mold**   bowls

whisk   kitchen scissors

pastry brush   vegetable peeler

1 1/2-inch round
cookie cutter

pastry bag and
medium star tube

saucepans

parchment paper

chopping board
** deep metal bowl can also be
used

*A winter dream come true for chocolate lovers –
half fudge, half cake, baked in a Charlotte mold,
then swathed with Chantilly cream and decorated
with chocolate coins and curls. If you don't have
time to make coins, mint sprigs or candied violets
make attractive alternatives.*

GETTING AHEAD

The charlotte can be prepared up to 1 week ahead and kept
in the refrigerator, or it can be frozen. The chocolate coins
can be layered with parchment paper and stored in the
refrigerator up to 1 week. Make the Chantilly cream and
decorate the charlotte not more than 2 hours before serving.

* plus 24 hours chilling time

SHOPPING LIST

4 oz	semisweet chocolate for coins
1	bar semisweet chocolate for curls
For the chocolate charlotte	
	butter for mold
8 oz	semisweet chocolate
3/4 cup	strong black coffee
1 cup	unsalted butter
1 cup	sugar
4	eggs
For the Chantilly cream	
1 1/2 cups	heavy cream
1 1/2 tbsp	sugar
3/4 tsp	vanilla extract

INGREDIENTS

semisweet chocolate

unsalted butter

heavy cream

eggs

strong black
coffee

vanilla extract

sugar

chocolate bar

ORDER OF WORK

1 MAKE THE
CHOCOLATE
CHARLOTTE

2 UNMOLD THE
CHARLOTTE

3 DECORATE THE
CHARLOTTE

1 MAKE THE CHOCOLATE CHARLOTTE

1 Brush the inside of the mold with melted butter. Line the bottom with a disk of parchment paper and butter the paper. Chill while preparing the mixture. Heat the oven to 350°F.

2 Cut the chocolate into large chunks. Chop them with the chef's knife, or in a food processor using the pulse button. Put the chocolate into a heavy-based medium saucepan, add the coffee, and heat, stirring with the wooden spoon, until the mixture is smooth and thick but still falls easily from the spoon, 5-7 minutes.

Sugar is added to butter and melted chocolate mixture

As soon as chocolate mixture comes to a boil, remove from heat

3 Cut the butter into pieces and add to the saucepan followed by the sugar. Heat, stirring, until the butter has melted and the sugar dissolved. Bring the mixture almost to a boil, stirring well with the wooden spoon.

4 Remove the saucepan from the heat and whisk in the eggs, one by one, whisking well after each addition.

ANNE SAYS
"*The eggs will cook and thicken in the heat of the mixture.*"

5 Strain the mixture into the prepared mold. Bake the charlotte in the heated oven until a thick crust forms on top, 45-55 minutes. Let cool, then cover and refrigerate at least 24 hours. The charlotte will shrink slightly on cooling.

ANNE SAYS
"*While still hot, the mixture will still be quite soft under the crust.*"

2 UNMOLD THE CHARLOTTE

1 Run the thin-bladed knife between the charlotte and the mold to loosen it from the mold.

2 Dip the base of the mold briefly into a pan of warm water, then lift it out and dry the mold.

3 Hold a serving plate over the mold, invert the plate and mold, then lift off the mold. Peel off the paper. Chill the charlotte until ready to decorate.

HOW TO MAKE CHOCOLATE COINS

Chocolate can be shaped into geometric decorations. Once set, they can be layered with parchment paper and stored in the refrigerator up to 1 week.

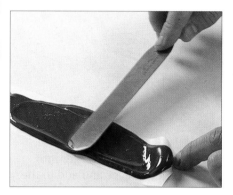

2 With a 1½-inch cookie cutter or the broad end of a piping tube, cut circles in the chocolate. Let set.

! TAKE CARE !
Do not refrigerate the coins before they are set because the chocolate will shrink away from the paper and buckle.

1 Cut a strip of parchment paper 12-inches long and 2-inches wide. Cut the chocolate into large chunks. Chop them with a chef's knife, or in a food processor using the pulse button. Melt the chocolate in a bowl set in a saucepan half-filled with hot water, then cool slightly. Spread the chocolate on the paper in an even layer about ¹/₁₆-inch thick. Let cool until on the point of setting.

ANNE SAYS
"For a shiny finish on the chocolate coins, temper the chocolate (see box, page 55) after melting it."

3 When the chocolate is firm, flip the paper strip over onto a sheet of parchment. Loosen the end of the strip with the tip of a small knife, then peel away paper. Remove the coins.

Use tip of small knife to lift chocolate coins

3 DECORATE THE CHARLOTTE

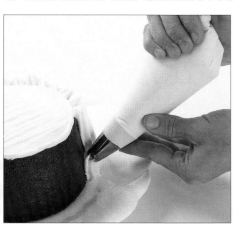

1 Use the 4 oz semisweet chocolate to make 8 chocolate coins (see box, page 70). Make the Chantilly cream: Pour the cream into a chilled bowl and whip until soft peaks form. Add the sugar and vanilla extract and continue whipping until stiff peaks form. Spread a little of the cream over the top of the charlotte using the metal spatula. Put the remaining cream into the pastry bag and pipe vertical lines to cover the side of the charlotte.

2 Pipe swirls of Chantilly cream around the base and top edge of the charlotte.

Squeeze pastry bag gently and evenly to pipe

3 With the vegetable peeler, make curls from the bar of semisweet chocolate. Sprinkle over the top. Arrange the chocolate coins around the base of the charlotte.

VARIATION

SMALL CHOCOLATE CHARLOTTES

These individual servings of Chocolate Charlotte are a fine finish for a winter dinner party.

1 Prepare the chocolate charlotte mixture as directed.
2 Line 8 medium ramekins (3/4-cup capacity) with foil and fill with the charlotte mixture.
3 Bake until crusty, 25-35 minutes, a little longer if necessary. Let cool, then refrigerate and unmold as directed.
4 Pipe stars of Chantilly cream all over the charlottes, using a small star tube, and decorate with chocolate coins, making double the number in the main recipe.

Fudgy chocolate charlotte is covered with piped Chantilly cream

Chocolate curls are a delicate finishing touch

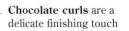

CHOCOLATE MOUSSE WITH HAZELNUTS AND WHISKEY

🍽 SERVES 6 🥄 WORK TIME 20-25 MINUTES ❄ CHILLING TIME AT LEAST 1-1½ HOURS

EQUIPMENT

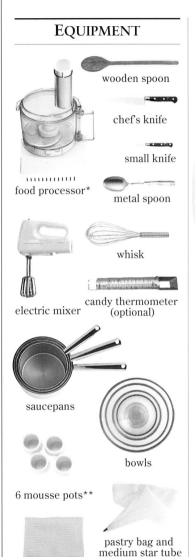

wooden spoon

chef's knife

small knife

food processor*

metal spoon

whisk

electric mixer

candy thermometer (optional)

saucepans

bowls

6 mousse pots**

pastry bag and medium star tube

dish towel

baking sheet   chopping board

rubber spatula

*blender can also be used

**stemmed glasses or ramekins can also be used

Toasted hazelnuts create texture, and whiskey gives zip, to this version of classic dark chocolate mousse. If you prefer, you can substitute almost any spirit or liqueur for the whiskey – rum, brandy, or Grand Marnier taste particularly good with chocolate.

GETTING AHEAD

The mousse can be made 1 day ahead and kept, covered, in the refrigerator. Decorate just before serving.

SHOPPING LIST

½ cup	hazelnuts
8 oz	semisweet chocolate
½ cup	water
1 tbsp	unsalted butter
3	eggs
2 tbsp	whiskey
¼ cup	sugar
	For the Chantilly cream
½ cup	heavy cream
1 tbsp	sugar
2 tsp	whiskey

INGREDIENTS

hazelnuts

semisweet chocolate

unsalted butter

eggs

heavy cream   whiskey

sugar

ANNE SAYS

"Cold mousse, with a frothy texture, is one of the most popular French desserts. Some mousses need gelatin to hold them; chocolate sets by itself. For a light mousse, the chocolate mixture and Italian meringue should be about the same consistency when folded together."

ORDER OF WORK

1 **MAKE THE MOUSSE MIXTURE**

2 **DECORATE THE MOUSSE**

MAKE THE MOUSSE MIXTURE

1 Toast and skin the hazelnuts (see box, below). Grind them in the food processor, reserving 6 whole nuts for decoration. Alternatively, use a rotary grater.

! TAKE CARE !
Do not overwork or the oil will be released from the nuts, creating a paste.

Process hazelnuts all at same time so they will be evenly ground

2 Cut the chocolate into large chunks. Chop them with the chef's knife, or in a food processor using the pulse button, then place in a medium heavy-based saucepan and add half of the water. Heat gently, stirring, until melted and the consistency of heavy cream, 3-5 minutes.

3 Remove the saucepan of melted chocolate from the heat and stir in the butter, cut in pieces.

4 Separate the eggs. Whisk the egg yolks into the chocolate mixture one by one, whisking well after each addition. Whisk the chocolate mixture over low heat about 4 minutes to ensure that the yolks are cooked.

HOW TO TOAST AND SKIN NUTS

Toasting nuts intensifies their flavor and adds crunch to their texture. It also loosens thin skin from nuts such as hazelnuts, so the skins can be removed easily by rubbing with a rough dish towel.

1 Heat the oven to 350° F. Spread the nuts on a baking sheet and bake until lightly browned, stirring occasionally so they color evenly.

! TAKE CARE !
Watch so the nuts do not burn or they will have a very bitter flavor.

2 To remove skins from hazelnuts, rub with a rough dish towel while still hot.

5 Remove from the heat and whisk in the hazelnuts and whiskey. Let the mixture cool to tepid.

HOW TO WHISK EGG WHITES UNTIL STIFF

Egg whites should be whisked until stiff but not dry. For egg whites to whisk properly, the whites, bowl, and whisk must be completely free from any trace of water, grease, or egg yolk. A copper bowl and a large balloon whisk are the classic French utensils used for whisking egg whites. A metal or glass bowl with a balloon whisk or electric mixer can also be used.

1 Begin whisking the whites slowly. When they are foamy and white, increase the whisking speed. If you like, add a small pinch of salt or cream of tartar to help achieve maximum volume.

! TAKE CARE !
Do not stop or slow down the whisking at this stage or the egg whites may "turn," becoming grainy and hard to fold into other ingredients.

2 The whites are whisked enough when they form a stiff peak when the whisk is lifted, gathering in the whisk wires and sticking without falling. The whites should be used at once because they separate quickly on standing.

! TAKE CARE !
Do not overbeat the egg whites; if they are overbeaten, the correct texture cannot be reconstituted.

Use small, deep saucepan for boiling sugar syrup

Hold saucepan firmly so stream of sugar syrup can be controlled

6 Put remaining water in a small pan, add the sugar, and heat until dissolved, stirring occasionally. Boil without stirring until syrup reaches 248°F on thermometer.

ANNE SAYS
"To test the syrup without a thermometer, take the pan from the heat, dip a teaspoon in the hot syrup, and remove it. Let the syrup cool a few seconds, then take a little between your finger and thumb: it should form a firm, pliable ball."

7 Meanwhile, whisk the egg whites until stiff (see box, above). Gradually pour in the hot sugar syrup, whisking constantly. Continue whisking until the meringue is cool and stiff, about 5 minutes.

ANNE SAYS
"To steady the bowl as you whisk, set it on a dish towel."

8 Stir one-quarter of the meringue into the tepid chocolate mixture.

9 Add the meringue and chocolate mixture to the remaining meringue and fold in gently.

2 DECORATE THE MOUSSE

1 Make the Chantilly cream: Pour the cream into a chilled bowl and whip until soft peaks form. Add the sugar and whiskey and continue whipping until stiff peaks form. Fill the pastry bag and star tube with the cream and decorate the top of each mousse with a single large rosette and a whole hazelnut.

ANNE SAYS
"If you prefer, chop the reserved hazelnuts and sprinkle onto the cream."

Divide mousse mixture equally among pots

10 Spoon the chocolate mousse into the mousse pots and chill until set, at least 1 hour.

Rosette of whipped cream, sweetened and flavored with whiskey

VARIATION
DOUBLE-CHOCOLATE MOUSSE
Chunks of white chocolate provide a color contrast in this variation.

1 Omit the hazelnuts and whiskey.
2 Coarsely chop 2 oz white chocolate or use 1/2 cup white chocolate chips.
3 Make the mousse as directed, and fold in three-quarters of the white chocolate before chilling.
4 Omit the Chantilly cream and sprinkle the mousse with the remaining white chocolate before serving.

CHOCOLATE SOUFFLE

¶❶❶ SERVES 4   **🥄** WORK TIME 20-25 MINUTES   **♨** BAKING TIME 15-18 MINUTES

EQUIPMENT

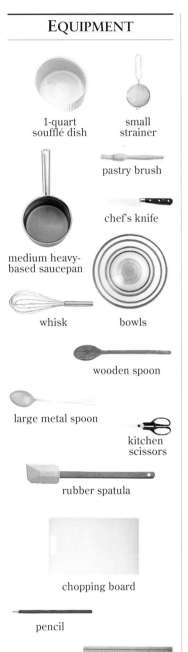

1-quart soufflé dish

small strainer

pastry brush

chef's knife

medium heavy-based saucepan

whisk

bowls

wooden spoon

large metal spoon

kitchen scissors

rubber spatula

chopping board

pencil

ruler

cardboard

My favorite soufflé: The chocolate is so thick and rich that it holds the whisked egg whites without any added flour. Be careful not to overcook the soufflé – the best part is the soft, creamy center that forms a sauce for the crisp outside. To serve a soufflé correctly, use 2 large metal spoons. Plunge them into the center of the soufflé and scoop out a wedge so each serving is partly firm, partly soft.

GETTING AHEAD
You can prepare the chocolate mixture for the soufflé through step 5 up to 3 hours before baking. Keep it, covered, in the refrigerator. Whisk the egg whites and fold them into the chocolate mixture just before baking.

SHOPPING LIST

	butter for dish
4 oz	semisweet chocolate
1/2 cup	heavy cream
3	eggs
2 tbsp	brandy
1/2 tsp	vanilla extract
2	egg whites
3 tbsp	granulated sugar
	For sprinkling
2-3 tbsp	confectioners' sugar

INGREDIENTS

eggs

semisweet chocolate

heavy cream

brandy

confectioners' sugar

egg whites

vanilla extract

granulated sugar

ANNE SAYS
"When baking a soufflé, set the dish low down in the oven so the soufflé has room to rise. If you open the oven door during baking to turn the dish so that it cooks evenly, the soufflé will not sink, but do avoid drafts."

ORDER OF WORK

1 PREPARE THE CHOCOLATE MIXTURE

2 BAKE THE CHOCOLATE SOUFFLE

1 PREPARE THE CHOCOLATE MIXTURE

1 Brush the soufflé dish with melted butter. Heat the oven to 425° F.

2 Cut the chocolate into large chunks. Chop them with the chef's knife, or in a food processor using the pulse button. Put the chocolate in the saucepan, add the cream, stir to mix, then heat gently, stirring, until melted and smooth, about 5 minutes.

Pour cream over chopped chocolate and stir to mix before placing over heat

3 If the mixture is a little thin, simmer it to the consistency of heavy cream. Remove the saucepan from the heat.

Check consistency of chocolate and cream mixture by lifting spoonful out of pan

4 Separate the eggs. Whisk the egg yolks into the hot mixture one by one, stirring well with the whisk after each addition. Whisk the chocolate mixture over low heat about 4 minutes to ensure that the egg yolks are cooked.

Whisk in each egg yolk before adding next so mixture stays smooth

5 Remove from the heat and whisk in the brandy and vanilla extract.

6 If necessary, reheat the chocolate mixture until hot to the touch. Whisk the 5 egg whites until stiff. Sprinkle in the sugar and continue whisking until glossy to form a light meringue, about 20 seconds. Cut and fold the meringue and chocolate mixtures together (see box, page 78).

HOW TO CUT AND FOLD 2 MIXTURES TOGETHER

Two mixtures can be folded together most easily if their consistency is similar. If one ingredient is much lighter or more liquid than the other, such as the light meringue and heavier chocolate and cream mixture in this soufflé, first stir a little of the lighter mixture into the heavier one to soften it.

1 Spoon one-quarter of the light mixture over the heavier mixture and stir in with a rubber spatula.

2 Add this mixture to the remaining meringue in the bowl.

Scoop under contents of bowl and bring spatula up, turning bowl counter-clockwise

Take spatula down into mixture, continuing to turn bowl counter-clockwise

Cut down into center of mixture with edge of spatula

Bring spatula round under mixture again, turning bowl counter-clockwise

3 With a rubber spatula, or a wooden or metal spoon, cut down into the center of the bowl, scoop under the contents and turn them over in a rolling motion. At the same time, turn the bowl counter-clockwise.

ANNE SAYS

"*This should be a synchronized movement: cut and scoop with the spatula in one hand, turn the bowl with the other. Using this method, the spatula reaches the maximum volume of mixture in one movement, so mixture is folded quickly and loses a minimum of air.*"

BAKE THE CHOCOLATE SOUFFLE

1 Gently pour the soufflé mixture into the prepared dish.

2 Carefully place the soufflé in the heated oven and bake until puffed, 15-18 minutes.

🍴 TO SERVE Make a template out of thin cardboard. Remove the soufflé from the oven and quickly place the template on top. Sprinkle with confectioners' sugar, using the strainer, then carefully remove the cardboard. Serve immediately.

V A R I A T I O N
INDIVIDUAL CHOCOLATE SOUFFLES

The chocolate soufflé mixture bakes well as individual servings.

1 Butter 4 large ramekins (1 cup capacity).
2 Prepare the chocolate mixture as directed in the main recipe.
3 Divide the mixture among the ramekins and bake 10-12 minutes.
4 Sprinkle with cocoa powder and confectioners' sugar and serve immediately, with crisp cookies, if you like.

V A R I A T I O N
AMARETTO CHOCOLATE SOUFFLE

Italian Amaretti cookies soaked in Amaretto liqueur are a delicious surprise in this soufflé.

1 Put 3-4 Amaretti cookies in a plastic bag and crush them with a rolling pin. Reserve for decoration.

2 Lay 14-16 more Amaretti cookies upside-down in a shallow dish and brush generously with 1/3 cup Amaretto liqueur.
3 Butter a 5-cup soufflé dish.
4 Prepare the chocolate mixture as directed, replacing the brandy with Amaretto liqueur.
5 Pour half of the mixture into the prepared dish, then lay the soaked cookies on top. Cover with the remaining soufflé mixture.
6 Bake the soufflé as directed in the main recipe.
7 Sprinkle with the crushed cookies and serve at once.

Place soufflé on serving plate for easy handling

STEAMED MEXICAN CHOCOLATE PUDDING WITH APRICOT SAUCE

🍽️ SERVES 6-8　　🥣 WORK TIME 20-25 MINUTES　　🍲 STEAMING TIME 60-70 MINUTES

EQUIPMENT

bowl strainer

conical strainer

chef's knife　　kitchen scissors

metal skewer

wooden spoon

ladle

deep 1-quart ceramic or glass pudding bowl

whisk

parchment paper

electric mixer

large pot with lid*

dish towel

saucepans

pastry brush

bowls

food processor**

rubber spatula

*steamer can also be used
**blender can also be used

INGREDIENTS

chocolate cake

semisweet chocolate

canned apricots

vanilla extract

sugar

unsalted butter

milk

eggs

kirsch

ground cinnamon

ground cloves

Christmas plum pudding is only the beginning of steamed pudding possibilities. The flavor of this steamed chocolate pudding is accentuated, Mexican-style, with cinnamon, while the apricot sauce and garnish provide a contrast in color.

GETTING AHEAD

The pudding and apricot sauce can be made up to 3 days ahead and refrigerated. Keep the pudding in the bowl and reheat it by steaming 30-40 minutes. Warm the sauce just before serving.

SHOPPING LIST

For the pudding batter	
6 oz	chocolate cake
1 tbsp	ground cinnamon
1 tsp	ground cloves
3 oz	semisweet chocolate
¾ cup	milk
	butter for pudding bowl
¼ cup	unsalted butter
¼ cup	sugar
2	eggs
½ tsp	vanilla extract
For the apricot sauce	
10 oz	canned apricots in syrup
1-2 tbsp	kirsch (optional)

ORDER OF WORK

1 PREPARE THE PUDDING BATTER

2 STEAM THE PUDDING

3 MAKE THE APRICOT SAUCE

1 PREPARE THE PUDDING BATTER

Shake food processor bowl and tap gently on edge of saucepan to release cake crumbs

1 Cut the cake into pieces and grind, a few pieces at a time, in the food processor to make crumbs. There should be about 2 cups. Stir in spices.

2 Cut the chocolate into large chunks. Chop them with the chef's knife, or in a food processor using the pulse button. Heat the chocolate with the milk in a heavy-based medium saucepan, stirring until melted and smooth. Bring the mixture to a boil and remove from the heat.

3 Add the spiced cake crumbs to the chocolate milk mixture. Stir well with the wooden spoon and let soak, 20-30 minutes.

4 Brush the pudding bowl with melted butter.

5 Using the electric mixer, cream the butter in a large bowl. Add the sugar and beat until fluffy and light, 2-3 minutes.

ANNE SAYS
"You can also cream the butter and sugar with a wooden spoon."

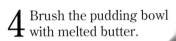

Add sugar to creamed butter while beating with electric mixer

6 Separate the eggs. Add the egg yolks to the butter mixture one by one, beating well after each addition.

7 Stir the soaked cake crumbs and vanilla into the creamed mixture until the batter is evenly blended.

8 Whisk the egg whites until stiff, then fold them into the chocolate batter mixture.

9 Pour the batter into the prepared pudding bowl, scraping it all in with the rubber spatula.

2 STEAM THE PUDDING

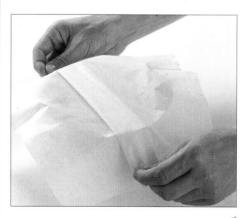

1 Pour enough water into the large pot to come about halfway up the side of the pudding bowl. Put a rack or upturned saucer on the bottom of the pot. Bring the water to a boil. Butter a sheet of parchment paper, pleat it in the center, and lay it over the bowl.

2 Lay the dish towel, also pleated in the center, on the paper and tie it securely under the lip of the bowl with kitchen string.

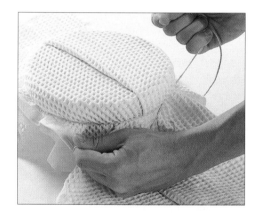

3 Knot the ends of the towel together. Trim off the excess parchment paper. Lift the bowl by the knotted towel, and lower it into the pot.

"Handle" made from knotted dish towel is convenient for lifting bowl in and out of pot

ANNE SAYS
"If the pudding is not done, wrap a piece of foil tightly over the bowl and continue cooking."

Insert skewer to test whether pudding is cooked

4 Steam the pudding 60-70 minutes. Lift the pudding from the pot. Cut the string and remove the dish towel and paper. The pudding is done if the skewer inserted in the center is hot to the touch when withdrawn after 30 seconds.

3 MAKE THE APRICOT SAUCE

Tip drained apricots straight from strainer into food processor bowl

1 Drain the apricots, reserving the syrup. Set aside 3 apricot halves and purée the remainder in the food processor.

2 Work the purée through the conical strainer into a saucepan, pressing with the ladle. Add a little of the reserved syrup to make a pourable sauce, then stir in the kirsch if you like. Gently warm the sauce.

🍴 TO SERVE
Unmold the pudding onto a serving dish and spoon some of the warm apricot sauce around. Arrange the reserved apricot halves on top of the pudding. Serve any remaining apricot sauce separately.

Apricots add color and make attractive flower pattern on top of pudding

Warm apricot sauce is perfect complement for hot steamed pudding spiced with cinnamon and cloves

---

V A R I A T I O N

STEAMED MEXICAN CHOCOLATE PUDDING WITH CHOCOLATE SAUCE

A rich, dark chocolate sauce takes the place of the apricot sauce in the main recipe for chocolate pudding.

1 Prepare and steam the pudding as directed.
2 Meanwhile, make the chocolate sauce: Chop 6 oz semisweet chocolate and heat it with ⅓ cup water and 2 tbsp sugar in a small saucepan over low heat, stirring until the chocolate is melted and the sugar has dissolved. Bring to a boil and cook, stirring, until thickened, 1-2 minutes.
3 Unmold the pudding onto a serving dish and serve with the chocolate sauce.

CHOCOLATE AND PEAR TARTLETS

Tartelettes Tante Katherine

🍽 MAKES 8 TARTLETS   🥣 WORK TIME 30-35 MINUTES*   🍲 BAKING TIME 25-30 MINUTES

EQUIPMENT

food processor**

bowl strainer

small knife

chef's knife

eight 4-inch tartlet molds

ladle

vegetable peeler

pastry brush

bowls

conical strainer

melon baller

baking sheet

plastic wrap

chopping board

waxed paper

whisk

metal spatula***

rolling pin

**blender can also be used
***pastry scraper can also be used

No wonder Katherine was the favorite aunt of our neighbors in Normandy. These tartlets are superbly flavored.

* plus about 30 minutes chilling time

SHOPPING LIST

5 oz	semisweet chocolate
2	large, ripe pears, total weight about 1½ lbs
1-2 tbsp	granulated sugar for sprinkling
	mint sprigs for decoration
	For the pastry dough
1½ cups	flour
6 tbsp	unsalted butter + extra for molds
⅓ cup	granulated sugar
½ tsp	salt
½ tsp	vanilla extract
3	egg yolks
	For the custard
1	egg
½ cup	light cream
1 tbsp	kirsch
	For the raspberry coulis
2 cups	raspberries (1 pint)
1-2 tbsp	kirsch (optional)
2-3 tbsp	confectioners' sugar

INGREDIENTS

pears

semisweet chocolate

flour

eggs

light cream

vanilla extract

kirsch

unsalted butter

granulated sugar

egg yolks

raspberries

confectioners' sugar

ORDER OF WORK

1 MAKE THE PASTRY DOUGH

2 LINE THE TARTLET MOLDS

3 FILL AND BAKE THE TARTLETS; MAKE THE COULIS

1 MAKE THE PASTRY DOUGH

1 Sift the flour onto a work surface, tapping the side of the strainer.

Sift flour to aerate it and make pastry light

Use fine-meshed strainer to remove any lumps from flour and tap with your hand on side to help flour sift through

2 Put the butter between 2 sheets of waxed paper and pound with the rolling pin to soften it slightly.

3 Make a well in the center of the flour with your hand.

4 Put the sugar, salt, and vanilla extract in the well.

Use tips of fingers so that ingredients are handled as lightly as possible

Softened butter blends easily with sugar

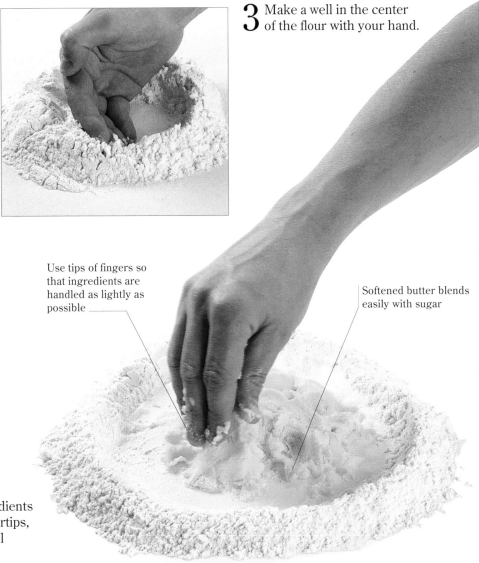

5 Add the butter to the ingredients in the well. With your fingertips, work the ingredients in the well until thoroughly mixed.

6 Add the egg yolks and work into the ingredients in the well. Draw in the flour with the metal spatula. With your fingers, work the flour into the other ingredients until coarse crumbs form. Press the dough into a ball.

Draw ingredients together with fingertips

Push flour into well little by little

Use metal spatula to scrape up dough from work surface

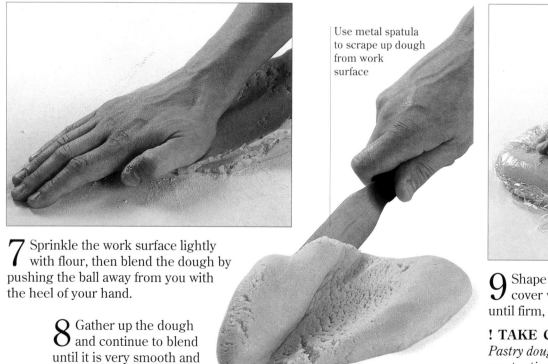

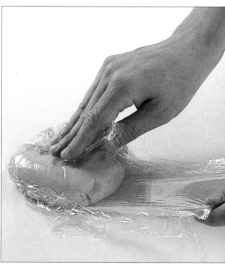

7 Sprinkle the work surface lightly with flour, then blend the dough by pushing the ball away from you with the heel of your hand.

8 Gather up the dough and continue to blend until it is very smooth and peels away from the work surface in one piece, 1-2 minutes.

9 Shape the dough into a ball again, cover with plastic wrap, and chill until firm, about 30 minutes.

! TAKE CARE !
Pastry doughs made with a lot of sugar are particularly delicate. Be sure to chill the dough before rolling out.

2 LINE THE TARTLET MOLDS

1 Brush the insides of the tartlet molds with melted butter. Group 4 of the tartlet molds together, with their edges nearly touching.

2 Sprinkle the work surface lightly with flour. Divide the ball of dough in half and roll it out to ⅛-inch thickness. Roll the dough loosely around the rolling pin and drape it over the 4 molds to cover them completely.

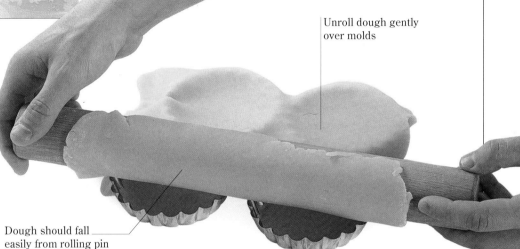

Unroll dough gently over molds

Dough should fall easily from rolling pin

3 Tear off a small piece of dough from the edge, form it into a ball, dip it in flour, and use it to push the dough into the molds.

4 Roll the rolling pin over the tops of the molds to cut off excess dough.

ANNE SAYS
"Excess dough can be rolled out again, and then used to line any remaining tartlet molds."

5 With your fingers, press the dough into the flutes of each mold to form a deep shell. Repeat with the 4 remaining molds and dough.

3 FILL AND BAKE THE TARTLETS; MAKE THE COULIS

1 Heat the oven to 400° F. Heat the baking sheet. Cut the chocolate into large chunks. Finely chop them with the chef's knife, or in a food processor using the pulse button. Sprinkle into each tartlet shell.

Scatter finely chopped chocolate evenly in tartlet shells

2 To make the custard, whisk the egg, cream, and kirsch together until thoroughly mixed.

3 Spoon about 2-3 tbsp of the kirsch custard over the chopped chocolate in each tartlet shell.

4 Peel the pears, cut them in half, and remove the cores with the melon baller. Cut out the stem end with the small knife.

ANNE SAYS
"To keep the pears from turning brown, sprinkle them with a little lemon juice."

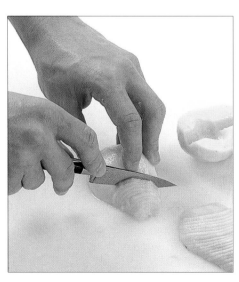

Lay pear slices in tartlet shells to resemble flower shape

5 With the small knife, cut each pear half crosswise into very thin slices.

6 Arrange the pear slices in a flower-petal design on the custard so that the slices overlap.

7 Press the pear slices down lightly into the custard, then sprinkle the pears evenly with the sugar.

8 Put the tartlet molds on the heated baking sheet near the bottom of the heated oven. Bake 10 minutes, then reduce the heat to 350° F and bake until the pastry is golden and the custard is set, 15-20 minutes longer.

ANNE SAYS
"*Putting the tartlet molds on a heated baking sheet ensures that the bases of the tartlet shells cook thoroughly.*"

9 Meanwhile, make the raspberry coulis: Pick over the berries, then purée them in the food processor. Add the kirsch, if using, then confectioners' sugar to taste and purée again. Strain to remove the seeds.

CHOCOLATE AND APPLE TARTLETS

Apples replace pears in these tartlets, with the added spice of cinnamon.

1 Prepare the pastry dough and line the tartlet molds as directed in the recipe for Chocolate and Pear Tartlets.
2 Peel and core 3 apples, total weight about 1 lb. Cut them into small chunks.
3 Heat about 2 tbsp unsalted butter in a large saucepan. Add the apple chunks and sprinkle them with 1-2 tbsp sugar and 2 tsp ground cinnamon. Sauté briskly until slightly softened and caramelized, stirring occasionally, 3-5 minutes.
4 Sprinkle the chopped chocolate into the tartlet shells and spoon the custard over the top.
5 Spread the apples on the custard, pressing them down lightly. Bake as directed.

— **GETTING AHEAD** —
The pastry dough can be made up to 2 days in advance and kept in the refrigerator, or it can be frozen. The tartlets can be kept 6-8 hours, but are best eaten the day they are baked.

TO SERVE
Let the tartlets cool slightly. Spoon the raspberry coulis onto individual plates. Unmold the tartlets, place on the coulis, and decorate with mint sprigs. Serve warm or at room temperature.

Mint sprig is an appealing decoration

PROFITEROLES WITH CHOCOLATE ICE CREAM

 SERVES 8   WORK TIME 25-30 MINUTES*   BAKING TIME 25-30 MINUTES

EQUIPMENT

saucepans

strainer

pastry bag with ³/₈-inch plain tube

small sharp knife

pastry brush

melon baller**

chef's knife

fork

wooden spoons

1-2 baking sheets

serrated knife

bowls

wire rack

chopping board

**small ice-cream scoop or 2 teaspoons can also be used

Light and airy choux pastry puffs are filled with my chocolate ice cream and topped with a hot chocolate sauce.

GETTING AHEAD

All the elements can be prepared ahead: The ice cream and sauce can be frozen up to 2 weeks, and the choux puffs can be kept in an airtight container 2-3 days. Assemble the profiteroles just before serving.

* plus time to make ice cream

SHOPPING LIST

³/₄ quantity	Chocolate Ice Cream (see page 106)
	For the choux pastry
	butter for baking sheet
³/₄ cup + 2 tbsp	flour
¹/₃ cup	unsalted butter
³/₄ cup	water
¹/₂ tsp	salt
3-4	eggs
	For the egg glaze
1	egg
¹/₂ tsp	salt
	For the chocolate sauce
12 oz	semisweet chocolate
1 cup	heavy cream
2 tbsp	Cognac (optional)

INGREDIENTS

semisweet chocolate

eggs

heavy cream

unsalted butter

flour

chocolate ice cream

Cognac

ORDER OF WORK

1 PREPARE THE CHOUX PASTRY

2 MAKE THE GLAZE; BAKE THE PUFFS

3 MAKE THE CHOCOLATE SAUCE AND FINISH THE PUFFS

1 PREPARE THE CHOUX PASTRY

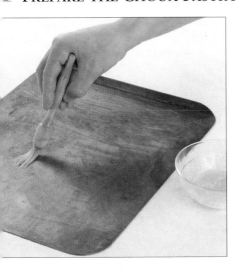

1 Heat the oven to 400°F. Brush the baking sheet evenly with melted butter. Sift the flour into a medium-sized bowl.

2 Cut the butter into pieces. Put them into a large saucepan with the water and salt.

Combine water and butter off the stove so they melt and blend together when heated

3 Heat until the butter has melted. Bring the mixture just to a boil. Remove from heat.

! TAKE CARE !
The water should not boil before the butter melts or the evaporation will change the dough proportions.

4 Add the flour to the butter mixture all at once and beat vigorously with a wooden spoon.

5 Beat until the mixture is smooth and pulls away from the side of the saucepan to form a ball of dough, about 20 seconds. Return the saucepan to the stove and beat over very low heat to dry out the ball of dough, about 30 seconds. Remove from heat.

Warmth of butter and water mixture cooks flour into ball of dough

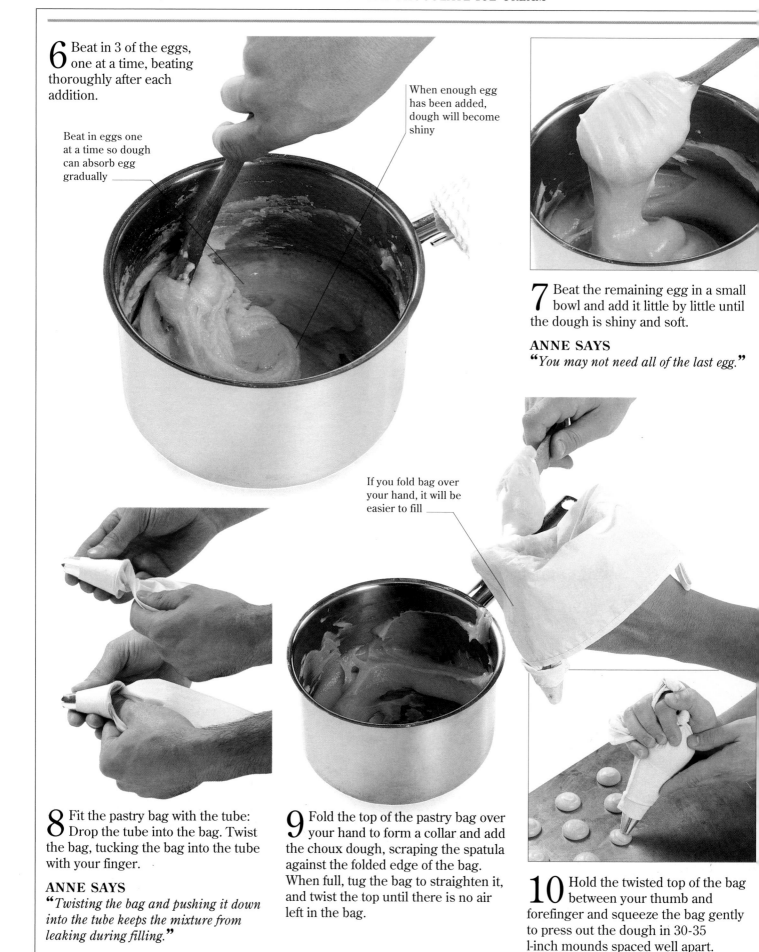

6 Beat in 3 of the eggs, one at a time, beating thoroughly after each addition.

Beat in eggs one at a time so dough can absorb egg gradually

When enough egg has been added, dough will become shiny

7 Beat the remaining egg in a small bowl and add it little by little until the dough is shiny and soft.

ANNE SAYS
"You may not need all of the last egg."

If you fold bag over your hand, it will be easier to fill

8 Fit the pastry bag with the tube: Drop the tube into the bag. Twist the bag, tucking the bag into the tube with your finger.

ANNE SAYS
"Twisting the bag and pushing it down into the tube keeps the mixture from leaking during filling."

9 Fold the top of the pastry bag over your hand to form a collar and add the choux dough, scraping the spatula against the folded edge of the bag. When full, tug the bag to straighten it, and twist the top until there is no air left in the bag.

10 Hold the twisted top of the bag between your thumb and forefinger and squeeze the bag gently to press out the dough in 30-35 l-inch mounds spaced well apart.

2 MAKE THE GLAZE; BAKE THE PUFFS

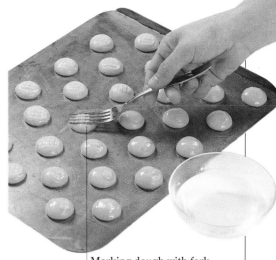

Marking dough with fork
helps it to rise evenly

1 Prepare the egg glaze: Beat the egg with the salt so they are well mixed. Leave 2-3 minutes until smooth and the salt softens the egg white.

2 Brush some egg glaze on each choux pastry puff.

! TAKE CARE !
Do not let any glaze fall on the baking sheet; it makes the dough stick and prevents it from rising evenly.

3 Press down lightly on each round with the tines of the fork, first in one direction and then in the other, to make a criss-cross pattern.

4 Bake the choux pastry puffs in the heated oven until the puffs are firm and brown, about 25-30 minutes. Transfer the choux puffs to the wire rack.

Folded dish towel is good stand-in for potholder

Each puff should be pleasantly rounded and golden brown

Egg glaze gives glossy finish

5 With small, sharp knife, make a horizontal slit in each puff to release steam. Let puffs cool. Meanwhile, if using ice cream made well ahead, let it soften in refrigerator.

3 MAKE THE CHOCOLATE SAUCE AND FINISH THE PUFFS

Stir constantly while heating chocolate and cream to prevent lumping

1 Chop the chocolate and put in a medium heavy-based saucepan with the cream. Heat gently, stirring with a wooden spoon, until the chocolate has melted and the mixture is smooth and thick.

2 If using Cognac, add it to the chocolate-and-cream mixture, and stir until evenly blended. Keep the sauce warm until ready to pour over the profiteroles.

Gently separate 2 halves of each profiterole to make room for ice cream

3 Fill each profiterole with a ball of ice cream. Pile the profiteroles in a shallow dish.

Chocolate ice cream peeps out of airy pastry puffs

🍴 TO SERVE
Pour the warm chocolate sauce over the profiteroles. Serve immediately.

Chocolate sauce is poured over filled profiteroles

VARIATION
CHOCOLATE ICE CREAM SWANS
Swans of choux pastry float on a lake of chocolate sauce in this elegant reworking of the profiterole theme.

1 Make the choux pastry as directed in the profiteroles recipe.

2 For 8-12 swan bodies, use a ⅝-inch plain tube in the pastry bag to pipe out ovals, about 1½ x 3 inches, onto a buttered baking sheet. Slightly elongate the ovals to form tails. Leave plenty of room for them to double in size while baking.
3 Hold a ¼-inch plain tube firmly over the first tube already in the pastry bag and pipe out 16 S-shaped necks with heads, 3-4 inches long, on a second buttered baking sheet (this number includes extra to allow for breakages).

4 Brush bodies and necks with egg glaze and bake as directed, allowing 10-15 minutes for the necks and 30-35 minutes for the bodies.
5 Transfer the baked bodies and necks to a wire rack. Cut the oval bodies in half horizontally with the serrated knife, then cut each top piece lengthwise in half for the wings. Allow to cool completely. Transfer the chocolate ice cream to the refrigerator to soften.
6 Make the chocolate sauce as directed in the profiteroles recipe.
7 Fill the bodies with balls of ice cream and insert a neck at the broad end. Arrange the wings in the ice cream at an angle so they spread up and out from the neck. Spoon pools of chocolate sauce onto individual plates. Sift 2-3 tbsp confectioners' sugar over the swans and set them on the plates. Serve immediately.

VARIATION
CHOUX CHANTILLY RING
Chocolate-speckled Chantilly cream fills this choux pastry ring.

1 Make the choux pastry as directed.
2 Using a ⅝-inch tube, pipe out an 8-inch-diameter ring onto a buttered baking sheet.

3 Pipe a second ring just inside the first. Pipe a third ring on top. Alternatively, spoon out the dough.
4 Brush with egg glaze and bake until firm and brown, 20-30 minutes. Transfer to a wire rack, split the ring horizontally to release the steam, and let cool completely.
5 Omit the chocolate ice cream. Make Chantilly cream: Whip 2 cups heavy cream in a chilled bowl until soft peaks form. Add 2 tbsp sugar and 1 tsp vanilla extract and continue whipping until stiff peaks form. Stir in 2 oz grated chocolate.
6 Spoon or pipe the chocolate-speckled cream onto the bottom of the cooled ring. Set the upper half on top.
7 Make the chocolate sauce as directed, let cool slightly, and drizzle a little over the ring using a paper piping cone or teaspoon. Fill the center of the ring with whole fresh strawberries. Serve immediately, with the remaining chocolate sauce handed separately.

BLACK AND WHITE CHOCOLATE MOUSSE TOWERS

🍽 SERVES 8 　🥄 WORK TIME 45-50 MINUTES 　❄ CHILLING TIME 30 MINUTES

EQUIPMENT

strainer

2 ½-inch round cookie cutter

food processor*

whisk

ladle

chopping board

saucepans

parchment paper

chef's knife

rubber spatula

bowls

pastry bag and large star tube

metal spatula

* blender can also be used

With a touch of art deco elegance, white chocolate mousse is layered with disks of dark chocolate, set on a brilliant background of raspberry coulis, and studded with fresh blueberries. To offset the sweetness of the mousse, blueberries are hidden within the sandwich – substitute raspberries if blueberries are not available. This dessert is such a crowd pleaser, that I've developed two delicious variations on the theme.

GETTING AHEAD

The chocolate disks can be layered with parchment paper and stored in the refrigerator up to 1 week. You can prepare the mousse, assemble the towers, and make the raspberry coulis 1 day ahead. Refrigerate them, and arrange on plates just before serving.

SHOPPING LIST

8 oz	semisweet chocolate
12 oz	white chocolate
1½ cups	heavy cream
½ pint	blueberries
	For the raspberry coulis
2 cups	raspberries
1-2 tbsp	kirsch (optional)
2-3 tbsp	confectioners' sugar

INGREDIENTS

white chocolate

semisweet chocolate

confectioners' sugar

blueberries　raspberries

heavy cream

kirsch

ANNE SAYS
"Drained, thawed frozen raspberries can be used for the coulis, but they lack the perfume of fresh berries."

ORDER OF WORK

1 MAKE THE CHOCOLATE DISKS

2 MAKE THE WHITE CHOCOLATE MOUSSE

3 ASSEMBLE THE TOWERS

4 FINISH THE DISH

1 MAKE THE CHOCOLATE DISKS

1 Cut the semisweet chocolate into large chunks. Chop them with the chef's knife, or in a food processor using the pulse button. Melt the chocolate in a large bowl set in a saucepan half-filled with hot water.

2 Cut 5 strips of parchment paper, each 15-inches long and 3-inches wide. Quickly spread the chocolate on the paper strips to an even layer about 1/8-inch thick. Let cool until on the point of setting.

ANNE SAYS
"It's a good idea to make extra strips of chocolate because the disks break easily."

Spread melted chocolate evenly with metal spatula

3 Using the cookie cutter, stamp out at least 24 disks. Let set.

ANNE SAYS
"You can also use a glass to cut the disks."

! TAKE CARE !
Do not refrigerate the disks before they set or the chocolate will shrink away from the paper and buckle.

4 When the chocolate is firm, turn the paper over and carefully peel the paper away from the disks, handling the shapes as little as possible so the chocolate does not melt and become dull. If the disks do not come off easily, re-cut them with the cookie cutter.

Use one hand to pull paper and other as guide

2 MAKE THE WHITE CHOCOLATE MOUSSE

Protect hands with cloth or pot holder

Set bowl on damp dish towel to hold it steady as you whisk

1 Chop the white chocolate and put it in a bowl. Bring half of the cream to a boil in a small saucepan and pour it over the chopped chocolate, whisking constantly until the chocolate has melted and is smooth. Let the mixture cool completely.

2 Whip the remaining cream until soft peaks form. Fold the whipped cream into the white chocolate mixture. Chill in the refrigerator until firm enough to pipe, about 30 minutes.

3 ASSEMBLE THE TOWERS

1 Make a berry coulis (see box, page 99) with the raspberries. Cover and chill the coulis in the refrigerator. Pick over the blueberries to remove all stems and any blemished fruit.

4 With your fingers, arrange a few blueberries in the center of the rosettes.

2 Fill the pastry bag and star tube with the white chocolate mousse.

3 Pipe out a circle of small mousse rosettes onto a chocolate disk.

ANNE SAYS
"You can spoon on the mousse instead of piping it."

Gently squeeze bag with one hand and use other as guide

Use very light pressure only

5 Set a chocolate disk on top and press it down gently with the end of the metal spatula.

6 Add another circle of mousse rosettes and fill with more blueberries.

Press chocolate with spatula rather than hands to prevent damage to disks

7 Cover with a third chocolate disk and decorate with a large central rosette of mousse. Top the rosette with a blueberry. Repeat with more disks, mousse, and blueberries to make a total of 8 towers.

HOW TO MAKE A BERRY COULIS

A coulis is a sauce of a thickish consistency, which can be savory or sweet, that is most usually made from fruits or vegetables. The word comes from "couloir", a type of antique French strainer. Fleshy fruits, such as berries, produce some of the best coulis. The sauce is the right thickness when it densely coats the back of a spoon.

1 Pick over raspberries, or hull strawberries or other berries, washing them only if they are dirty. Put the berries in a food processor.

3 Add liqueur, if you like, then add confectioners' sugar to taste. Purée again until the sugar is evenly blended with the berries.

2 Work the berries in the machine until they are puréed.

Only fine strainer will catch raspberry seeds

Use ladle only to assist sauce through strainer

4 For raspberries, work the puréed fruit through a fine strainer to remove the seeds.

4 FINISH THE DISH

1 Ladle a little raspberry coulis onto individual plates.

Use small ladle to help control amount of coulis

Plates with well in center allow coulis to "pool" in middle and give neat finishing edge

2 Tip the plates slightly; the sauce will spread evenly over the well in the center.

3 With the metal spatula, carefully transfer the towers to the plates.

Try to place tower exactly in center of plate

Gently slide tower off spatula with your fingertips

Use metal spatula so chocolate remains cool and is unaffected by heat of your hand

🍴 **TO SERVE**
Arrange the remaining blueberries in a ring around each chocolate mousse tower.

White chocolate mousse looks dainty piped in tiny rosettes on chocolate disks

Whole blueberries are placed at regular intervals around chocolate tower to create pretty "frame"

Raspberry coulis has been strained to give smooth, glossy finish

DARK CHOCOLATE WHISKEY MOUSSE TOWERS

When a mousse of dark chocolate replaces the white in Black and White Chocolate Mousse Towers, the flavor is even more intense.

1 Chop 8 oz semisweet chocolate, then melt in a saucepan with 1/4 cup water. Remove from the heat and stir in 1 tbsp unsalted butter, cut into pieces.
2 Separate 3 eggs. Whisk the yolks into the chocolate mixture, one by one. Whisk the mixture over low heat, about 4 minutes to ensure yolks are cooked.
3 Remove from the heat and whisk in 2 tbsp whiskey. Let cool until tepid.
4 Dissolve 1/4 cup sugar in 1/4 cup water, then boil without stirring to 248° F on a candy thermometer (the hard-ball stage). Whisk the egg whites until stiff and gradually whisk in the hot sugar syrup. Continue whisking until the meringue is cool and stiff, about 5 minutes.
5 Fold the meringue into the cooled chocolate mixture.
6 Make the dark chocolate disks as directed.
7 Substitute the dark chocolate mousse for the white chocolate mousse and assemble the towers as directed, spooning on the mousse rather than piping it.
8 Serve the towers on a pool of light cream surrounded by blueberries.

MARBLED BLACK AND WHITE CHOCOLATE MOUSSE TOWERS

Contrasting feathers of white on the dark chocolate squares give these mousse towers an art nouveau rather than an art deco look.

1 Chop 1 oz white chocolate and melt it as directed.

2 Make a paper piping cone (see box, page 34). Fill it with the melted white chocolate, fold the top to seal, and trim the tip.

3 Melt the dark chocolate. With a metal spatula, spread it evenly on each of four 2½- x 15-inch strips of parchment paper. Make feathered chocolate squares (see box, right).

4 Chill the squares until firm, then lift the squares from the paper with the metal spatula. Make the mousse.

5 Assemble the towers as directed, using raspberries instead of blueberries, and serve on the raspberry coulis.

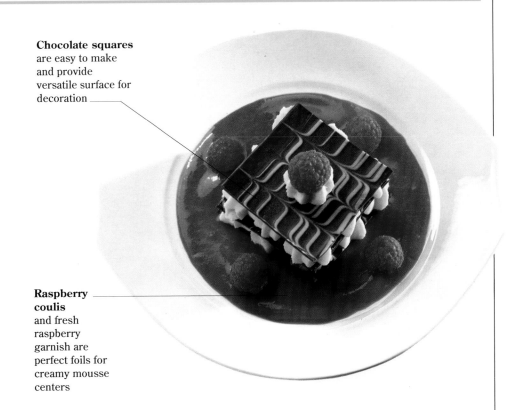

Chocolate squares are easy to make and provide versatile surface for decoration

Raspberry coulis and fresh raspberry garnish are perfect foils for creamy mousse centers

Place whole raspberry in center of mousse rosettes

HOW TO MAKE FEATHERED CHOCOLATE SQUARES

1 Pipe even lengthwise lines of melted white chocolate over one strip of dark chocolate, about ¼-inch apart.

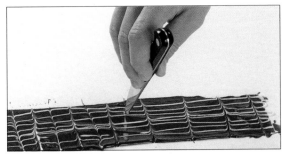

2 Draw the tip of a small knife crosswise through the white chocolate, first in one direction and then in the other, to create feathers. Repeat with the remaining chocolate strips. Let stand until almost set, 25-30 minutes.

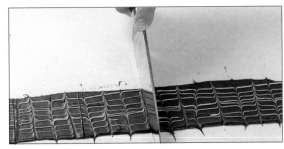

3 With a large knife, trim the edges of the chocolate strips if necessary and cut them across at 2½-inch intervals, making a total of 24 squares.

CHOCOLATE MOCHA SORBET

EQUIPMENT

ice-cream maker

rubber spatula

bowls

kitchen scissors

chef's knife

parchment paper

metal spatula

saucepans

metal spoons

wooden spoon

pencil

chopping board

tape

white paper

I think you'll like the surprisingly creamy texture of this sorbet, in which coffee combines with chocolate for the popular taste of mocha. Shaped into ovals (or "quenelles" as they are called in France), the sorbet looks particularly attractive served on individual plates. Homemade chocolate fans add an elegant finishing touch. If you are short of time, you can leave the sorbet plain, or use chocolate coffee beans as a complementary decoration instead.

GETTING AHEAD

The sorbet can be stored in the freezer up to 1 week, but the texture may coarsen. The chocolate fans can be layered with parchment paper and stored in the refrigerator up to 1 week.

* plus time to make chocolate fans

SHOPPING LIST

3 oz	unsweetened chocolate
3 cups	water
2-3 tbsp	instant coffee powder
1½ cups	sugar
3 oz	semisweet chocolate for chocolate fans

INGREDIENTS

unsweetened and semisweet chocolate

instant coffee powder

sugar

ANNE SAYS
"*Mocha is a term used to describe many coffee-and-chocolate-flavored dishes. Coffee's role as a flavor is small but important, and coffee can actually take the place of chocolate in many desserts. For flavoring, a dark roast is best. Instant coffee is the easiest form for adding coffee flavoring because it dissolves. You can also infuse a liquid such as milk with ground coffee beans, heat and let stand, then strain.*"

ORDER OF WORK

1 MAKE THE SORBET AND FANS

2 SHAPE THE SORBET FOR SERVING

1 MAKE THE SORBET AND FANS

Stirring with wooden spoon ensures sugar is evenly distributed and mixture does not stick

1 Cut the unsweetened chocolate into large chunks. Chop them with the chef's knife, or in a food processor using the pulse button. Put half of the water in a medium heavy-based saucepan, add the chopped chocolate and the coffee, and heat, stirring, until melted and smooth.

2 Add the sugar and the remaining water and heat, stirring, until the sugar has dissolved.

3 Bring to a boil and simmer 8-10 minutes, stirring – the mixture should thicken very slightly. Remove from the heat and let cool completely.

4 Pour the sorbet mixture into the ice-cream maker and freeze until slushy, following the manufacturer's directions. Meanwhile, chill a large bowl in the freezer.

Make sure sorbet mixture is completely cold before pouring into ice-cream maker

5 Transfer the sorbet to the chilled bowl, cover it, and freeze at least 4 hours to allow the flavor to mellow. Meanwhile, make 12-16 chocolate fans (see box, page 104).

ANNE SAYS
"Freezing time varies greatly with the machine you use."

HOW TO MAKE PIPED CHOCOLATE SHAPES

Melted chocolate can be piped into initials, fans, or baroque curlicues that, when set, can be removed from the paper and used to decorate ices and other desserts.

1 Draw or trace the desired shapes on a sheet of white paper. Tape a sheet of semi-transparent parchment paper to the work surface so it holds, then slide the drawing under the parchment paper.

Press hard with pencil so drawing will show through when under parchment paper

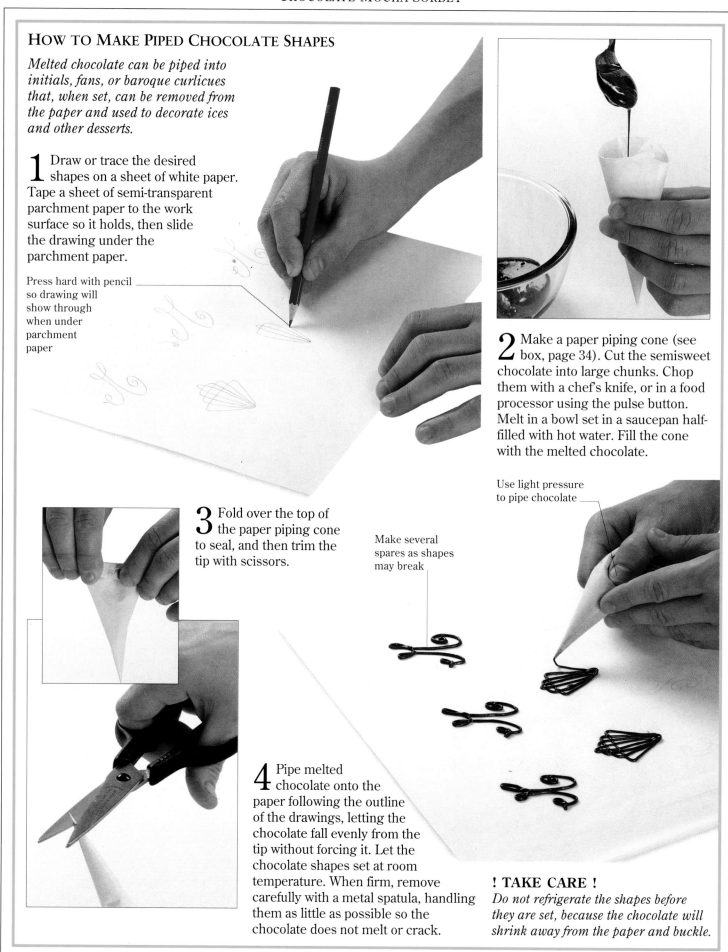

2 Make a paper piping cone (see box, page 34). Cut the semisweet chocolate into large chunks. Chop them with a chef's knife, or in a food processor using the pulse button. Melt in a bowl set in a saucepan half-filled with hot water. Fill the cone with the melted chocolate.

3 Fold over the top of the paper piping cone to seal, and then trim the tip with scissors.

Make several spares as shapes may break

Use light pressure to pipe chocolate

4 Pipe melted chocolate onto the paper following the outline of the drawings, letting the chocolate fall evenly from the tip without forcing it. Let the chocolate shapes set at room temperature. When firm, remove carefully with a metal spatula, handling them as little as possible so the chocolate does not melt or crack.

! TAKE CARE !
Do not refrigerate the shapes before they are set, because the chocolate will shrink away from the paper and buckle.

2 SHAPE THE SORBET FOR SERVING

1 Dip 2 metal spoons in cold water. Use one spoon to scoop out a generous spoonful of sorbet, then use the other spoon to shape the mixture into a neat 3-sided oval, turning the spoons one against the other. Repeat with the remaining sorbet to make 18-24 ovals altogether.

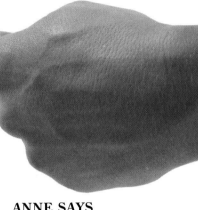

Transfer sorbet from one spoon to another to create smooth oval shape

ANNE SAYS
"If the sorbet has been frozen for more than 12 hours, it will need to soften 15-20 minutes in the refrigerator before shaping for serving."

🍴 **TO SERVE**
Arrange 3 ovals of sorbet on chilled individual plates and decorate with chocolate fans. Serve immediately.

Sorbet ovals look mouthwatering

Chocolate fans are elegant decoration

VARIATION
CHOCOLATE SORBET
This is one of the world's simplest chocolate desserts – light but intensely flavored. Serve it with your favorite wafer cookie.

1 Make and freeze the sorbet as directed, omitting the instant coffee powder.
2 Scoop balls of sorbet from the bowl with an ice-cream scoop and place on a chilled baking sheet lined with parchment paper.
3 Immediately place the baking sheet in the freezer and chill until the sorbet hardens.
4 To serve, lift the scoops of sorbet off the paper with a metal spatula and arrange in individual glass dishes. Serve immediately.

CHOCOLATE ICE CREAM

¶◉¶ MAKES 1 QUART TO SERVE 6-8 ⋓ WORK TIME 15-20 MINUTES ❄ FREEZING TIME 4-6 HOURS

EQUIPMENT

chef's knife

vegetable peeler

rubber spatula

wooden spoon

bowls   strainer

dish towel

heavy-based
medium
saucepan

ice-cream
maker

whisk

chopping board

parchment paper

ice-cream scoop

Homemade ice cream still beats them all, and chocolate is without doubt the number-one favorite flavor. Here, chocolate curls add a decorative touch. I leave you to choose your own accompaniment – ladyfingers or other cookies, or a colorful assortment of sliced fresh fruit in season.

GETTING AHEAD

The ice cream can be made up to 2 weeks ahead and kept in the freezer. It will be very hard, so let it soften in the refrigerator 30-60 minutes before serving.

SHOPPING LIST

8 oz	semisweet chocolate
2 ½ cups	milk
½ cup + 2 tbsp	sugar
8	egg yolks
2 tbsp	cornstarch
1 cup	heavy cream
1	bar covering (couverture) or semisweet chocolate for chocolate curls

INGREDIENTS

semisweet chocolate

sugar

egg yolks   heavy cream

cornstarch

milk

bar covering (couverture)
or semisweet chocolate

ANNE SAYS

"You will not use the entire bar of chocolate to make the curls for the decoration, but you will need a good-sized bar to be able to make them."

ORDER OF WORK

1 MAKE THE CHOCOLATE CUSTARD SAUCE

2 FREEZE THE ICE CREAM

MAKE THE CHOCOLATE CUSTARD SAUCE

1 With the chef's knife, cut the semisweet chocolate into large chunks. Chop them with the chef's knife, or in a food processor using the pulse button.

2 Put the milk in the saucepan, add the chopped chocolate, and heat, stirring, until melted and smooth.

Large chef's knife makes for easy chopping

Chocolate is chopped so it will melt easily in milk

Add chocolate to milk all at once

3 Add the sugar to the chocolate milk and stir until it has dissolved.

Whisk slowly so bubbles do not form

4 In a medium bowl, whisk the egg yolks with the cornstarch.

5 Gradually add three-quarters of the chocolate milk to the egg-yolk mixture, whisking slowly until smooth. Reserve the remaining chocolate milk in a measuring cup.

! TAKE CARE !
Do not overwhisk or the custard will be frothy instead of smooth.

Steady bowl on work surface with folded dish towel as you whisk

6 Return the mixture to the saucepan and cook over medium heat, stirring constantly with the wooden spoon, until the custard just comes to a boil and thickens enough to coat the back of the spoon. Let cool 1-2 seconds, then lift the spoon out of the custard and run your finger across the spoon: It should leave a clear trail.

! TAKE CARE !
Do not continue to boil the custard once it has thickened or it may curdle.

Pour custard through strainer to remove any bits of cooked egg yolk

7 Stir the reserved chocolate milk into the chocolate custard. Strain the chocolate custard sauce into a cold bowl and let cool. If the custard sauce forms a skin, whisk to dissolve it.

2 FREEZE THE ICE CREAM

1 Pour the chocolate custard sauce into the ice-cream maker and freeze until slushy, following manufacturer's directions. Meanwhile, chill 2 large bowls in the freezer.

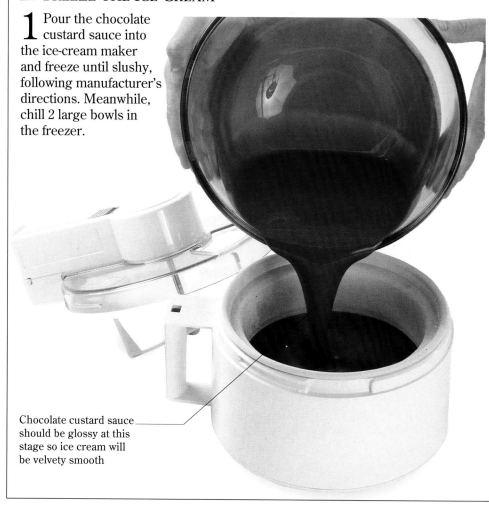

Chocolate custard sauce should be glossy at this stage so ice cream will be velvety smooth

2 Pour the cream into 1 chilled bowl and whip until it forms peaks and holds its shape.

3 Add the whipped cream to the partially-set chocolate custard and continue freezing until firm.

ANNE SAYS
"You'll find that the freezing time for the ice cream varies very much with the machine you use."

4 Transfer the ice cream to the second chilled bowl, cover, and freeze at least 4 hours.

🍴 TO SERVE

Make the chocolate curls: With the vegetable peeler, shave curls from the edge of the chocolate bar onto the parchment paper. Use the ice-cream scoop to form the ice cream into balls and divide among dessert bowls. Sprinkle chocolate curls on top.

Chocolate curls are sprinkled over scoops of ice cream

Ladyfingers add crisp contrast to velvety smooth ice cream

VARIATION

CHOCOLATE INDULGENCE ICE CREAM

An indulgence indeed, with two kinds of chopped chocolate added to Chocolate Ice Cream.

1 Coarsely chop 4 oz semisweet chocolate and 4 oz white chocolate. Alternatively, you can use equal portions of semisweet chocolate chips and white chocolate chips.
2 Make the chocolate ice cream as directed, adding the chopped chocolates with the whipped cream.
3 Serve scoops of ice cream, decorated with soft fruits, such as raspberries, and fresh mint sprigs.

VARIATION

CHOCOLATE PRALINE ICE CREAM

When praline is added to Chocolate Ice Cream, the result is crunchy and sweet with a slight tang, the best of all worlds.

1 Make the praline: Lightly oil a marble slab or baking sheet. Heat 1 1/4 cups whole unblanched almonds and 3/4 cup sugar in a heavy-based pan until the sugar melts, stirring with a wooden spoon. Continue cooking over fairly low heat to a medium caramel, stirring lightly. The sugar should be a deep golden brown and the almonds should make a popping sound.
2 Immediately pour the mixture onto the slab or baking sheet; spread out with the wooden spoon and leave until cool and crisp, 10-15 minutes.

3 Put the praline into a plastic bag and crack into pieces with a rolling pin, then coarsely grind in a food processor or blender.
4 Make the chocolate ice cream as directed. Reserve some praline for garnish and add the remainder to the ice cream with the whipped cream. Serve scooped into balls, with the reserved praline sprinkled on top.

CHEF FERRE'S FROZEN TRI-CHOCOLATE TERRINE

🍽 MAKES 12-16 SLICES   🥄 WORK TIME 35-40 MINUTES   ❄ FREEZING TIME 6-12 HOURS

EQUIPMENT

large terrine mold (about 12 x 3 x 3 inches)

kitchen scissors

chef's knife

pastry brush

bowls

whisk*

wooden spoon

parchment paper

strainer

rubber spatula

wooden rolling pin without handles

saucepans

roasting pan

chopping board

*electric mixer can also be used

Maurice Ferré has been the pastry chef at Maxim's in Paris for more than 35 years. His frozen chocolate terrine, composed of three sumptuously-flavored chocolate layers and sliced to serve with a pool of delicate mint custard sauce, is world famous.

INGREDIENTS

eggs

heavy cream

egg whites

semisweet chocolate

white chocolate

milk chocolate

milk

sugar

unsalted butter

egg yolks

cornstarch

fresh mint

SHOPPING LIST

	vegetable oil for mold
	For the chocolate layers
4 oz	semisweet chocolate
9 tbsp	heavy cream
6	eggs
9 tbsp	unsalted butter
6	egg whites
3 tbsp	sugar
5 oz	white chocolate
5 oz	milk chocolate
	For the mint custard sauce
1	bunch of fresh mint
2 cups	milk
1/3 cup	sugar
6	egg yolks
1½ tbsp	cornstarch

ORDER OF WORK

1 MAKE THE DARK CHOCOLATE LAYER

2 MAKE THE WHITE AND MILK CHOCOLATE LAYERS

3 MAKE THE MINT CUSTARD SAUCE

4 UNMOLD THE TERRINE

1 MAKE THE DARK CHOCOLATE LAYER

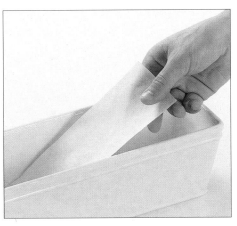

1 Using the pastry brush, lightly oil the sides and bottom of the mold.

ANNE SAYS
"If you like, you can rub the oil onto the mold with paper towel."

2 Using the base of the mold as a guide, draw and then cut out 2 strips of parchment paper. Use one to line the bottom of the mold and reserve the other.

3 Cut the semisweet chocolate into large chunks. Chop them with the chef's knife, or in a food processor using the pulse button. Melt the chocolate in a large bowl set in a saucepan half-filled with hot water.

4 In a small saucepan, bring 3 tbsp of the heavy cream just to boiling point, then whisk it into the melted chocolate.

Whisk constantly while adding cream so it mixes smoothly into chocolate

Mix in each batch of butter completely before adding more

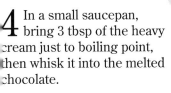

5 Separate 2 of the eggs. Whisk the egg yolks into the chocolate mixture one by one, stirring well before adding the second yolk.

6 Cut 3 tbsp of the butter into small pieces and add, a few pieces at a time, whisking so the butter melts smoothly into the warm mixture.

7 In another large bowl, whisk 4 of the egg whites until stiff.

ANNE SAYS
"If using an electric mixer, beat the whites on medium speed until they become foamy and white, then increase the speed to maximum."

Whisk whites until stiff peaks form

8 Sprinkle in 1 tbsp of the sugar and whisk until glossy, about 20 seconds, to make a light meringue.

Dark chocolate mixture forms top layer when terrine is turned out

9 Fold the meringue into the chocolate mixture as lightly as possible. This can be done in 2 batches, if you like.

10 Pour the dark chocolate mixture into the terrine.

! TAKE CARE !
Made this way, the terrine contains uncooked eggs. You can, if you like, cook the chocolate mixture over low heat about 4 minutes, whisking constantly, to ensure that the eggs are thoroughly cooked, with no danger of salmonella contamination. However, the terrine will be less fluffy and light.

Scrape inside of bowl to remove all mixture

11 Spread the chocolate mixture in the terrine, pushing it into the corners and smoothing the top evenly. Freeze 30-40 minutes while preparing the remaining layers.

2 MAKE THE WHITE AND MILK CHOCOLATE LAYERS

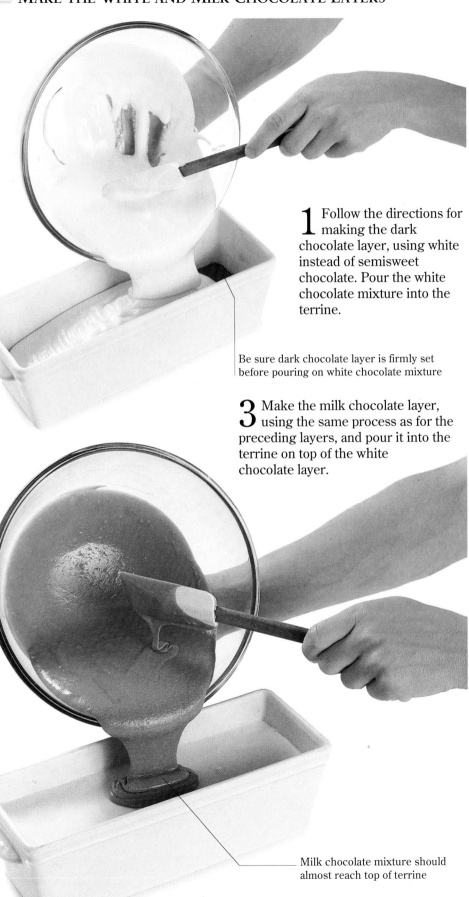

1 Follow the directions for making the dark chocolate layer, using white instead of semisweet chocolate. Pour the white chocolate mixture into the terrine.

Be sure dark chocolate layer is firmly set before pouring on white chocolate mixture

2 Spread over the dark chocolate layer and freeze, 30-40 minutes.

3 Make the milk chocolate layer, using the same process as for the preceding layers, and pour it into the terrine on top of the white chocolate layer.

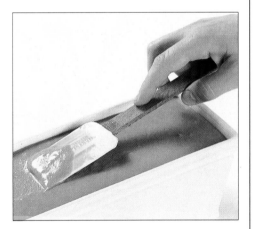

4 Smooth the top layer using the rubber spatula.

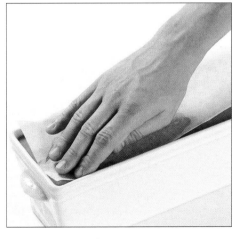

Milk chocolate mixture should almost reach top of terrine

5 Lightly press the reserved piece of parchment paper on top of the milk chocolate layer. Chill the terrine in the freezer until firm, at least 6 hours.

3 MAKE THE MINT CUSTARD SAUCE

1 Rinse the mint and trim the ends of the stems. Reserve 12-16 sprigs for decoration and lightly crush the remainder using the rolling pin.

Press down and rotate end of pin to bruise and soften mint leaves

Make sure prettiest sprigs are set aside for decoration

Reserve pan as sauce will be returned to it but wipe out any remaining mint

2 Put the milk in a heavy-based saucepan and bring just to a boil. Add the crushed mint, cover, and let infuse in a warm place 10-15 minutes.

3 Strain the milk into a glass measure or bowl and discard the crushed mint. Stir in the sugar until dissolved.

Use conical strainer to direct liquid into measure

4 Whisk the egg yolks with the cornstarch in a medium bowl. Add the infused milk, reserving about ½ cup. Whisk until just smooth, then return the custard to the saucepan.

Whisk only until custard is smooth or it will be too frothy

5 Cook over medium heat, stirring constantly with the wooden spoon, until the custard just comes to a boil and thickens enough to coat the back of the spoon. (Your finger will leave a clear trail across the spoon.) Stir in the reserved milk. Strain the custard into a chilled bowl and let cool.

4 UNMOLD THE TERRINE

1 Fill the roasting pan with hot water. Dip the base of the terrine into the hot water 10-15 seconds, then lift it out and dry it. Peel off the parchment from the top.

2 Set a rectangular serving dish or tray on top of the terrine and turn them over together. Remove the mold.

ANNE SAYS
"If the terrine sticks to the mold, run a knife dipped in hot water around the sides, between the terrine and the mold."

Parchment paper peels away easily from terrine

3 Peel off the paper. Let the terrine soften in the refrigerator about 1 hour before cutting it into ¾- to 1-inch-thick slices. Serve with mint custard sauce and mint sprig decoration.

Mint custard sauce should be served on the side

VARIATION

TRI-CHOCOLATE TERRINE ON STRAWBERRY COULIS

The vibrant color and taste of strawberry provide natural foils for the rich chocolate in Chef Ferré's Tri-Chocolate Terrine.

1 Make the terrine as directed and freeze.

2 Omit the mint custard sauce and instead prepare a strawberry coulis: Hull 1 quart strawberries, washing them only if they are dirty, then purée them in a food processor or blender. Add 2 tbsp kirsch, if desired, and 2-3 tbsp confectioners' sugar, then purée again.

3 Slice the terrine, then place the slices on individual plates. Cut each slice diagonally in half, and separate the halves slightly. Spoon strawberry coulis in between, and decorate with halved strawberries.

Mint sprig is perfect decoration

— GETTING AHEAD —
The terrine can be made up to 2 weeks ahead and frozen. The mint custard sauce can be made 1 day ahead and stored in the refrigerator.

CHOCOLATE AND APRICOT BOMBE

🍽 SERVES 6-8   🥄 WORK TIME 40-45 MINUTES*   ❄ FREEZING TIME 9-12 HOURS

EQUIPMENT

ice-cream maker

rubber spatula

bowls   strainer

saucepans

whisk**

wooden spoon

1½-quart bombe mold***

candy thermometer (optional)

metal spatula

chef's knife

chopping board

pastry bag and medium star tube

parchment paper

**electric mixer can also be used
***deep metal bowl can be used

A bombe was once spherical, hence its name. Now it usually has a flat base and is molded in layers with a rich, creamy center. This apricot filling, flavored with complementary kirsch, is so good that no one will notice if, to save time, you enclose it in store-bought instead of homemade chocolate ice cream.

* plus time to make ice cream

SHOPPING LIST

½ quantity	Chocolate Ice Cream (see page 106)
2 oz	semisweet chocolate for chocolate triangles
For the apricot bombe mixture	
4 oz	dried apricots
4	egg yolks
1 cup	granulated sugar
¼ cup	water
2-3 tbsp	kirsch
½ cup	heavy cream
For the chocolate fudge sauce	
4 oz	semisweet chocolate
½ cup	water
¼ cup	unsalted butter
2 tbsp	light brown sugar
	salt
To finish	
½ cup	heavy cream
2 tsp	granulated sugar
	canned apricots for garnish (optional)

INGREDIENTS

dried apricots   semisweet chocolate

egg yolks   light brown sugar

granulated sugar

kirsch

unsalted butter

heavy cream

chocolate ice cream

canned apricots

ORDER OF WORK

1   **LINE THE MOLD AND PREPARE THE APRICOT FILLING**

2   **MAKE THE CHOCOLATE TRIANGLES**

3   **MAKE THE CHOCOLATE FUDGE SAUCE**

4   **UNMOLD AND DECORATE THE BOMBE**

1 LINE THE MOLD AND PREPARE THE APRICOT FILLING

Try to spread ice cream in even layer so bombe looks neat when cut

1 Chill the bombe mold in the freezer. With the rubber spatula, spread the ice cream over the bottom and up the side of the mold in a 1- to 2-inch layer, leaving a neat, even hollow in the center. Freeze until firm, 30-60 minutes.

ANNE SAYS
"To be spreadable, the ice cream must be soft. Homemade ice cream should be used directly after freezing in the ice-cream maker. If made ahead, let it soften in the refrigerator about 30 minutes."

2 With the chef's knife, chop the dried apricots into small pieces. Put them into a small bowl and cover with boiling water. Let soak 15-20 minutes.

Chill bombe mold so ice cream does not melt

3 Put the egg yolks in a large bowl and whisk until just mixed.

4 Heat the sugar and water in a small pan until dissolved. Boil until the syrup reaches the soft-ball stage, 239°F on the candy thermometer. Gradually pour the syrup into the egg yolks, whisking constantly.

ANNE SAYS
"To test the syrup without a thermometer, take the pan from the heat. Dip a teaspoon in the hot syrup and take a little between your finger and thumb — it should form a soft ball."

As sugar syrup is whisked into egg yolks, mixture becomes thick and increases in volume

5 Continue whisking at high speed until the mixture is cool, very thick, and pale, about 5 minutes.

6 Turn the apricots into the strainer and drain off the liquid.

7 Return the apricots to the small bowl. Add the kirsch and mix well with the apricots.

8 Pour the cream into a bowl set in a larger bowl of ice water. Whip until it just holds its shape.

Rubber spatula is good for mixing ingredients together well

9 Add the apricot mixture to the egg yolk and sugar mixture and stir together.

10 Add the whipped cream to the apricot bombe mixture. Fold the cream into the mixture: Cut down into the center of the bowl, scoop under the contents and turn them over in a rolling motion. At the same time, with your other hand, turn the bowl counter-clockwise.

11 Remove the ice-cream-lined mold from the freezer and pour in the apricot bombe mixture.

ANNE SAYS
"If the apricots have sunk to the bottom of the cream mixture, stir well before pouring it into the mold."

12 Use the metal spatula to press the mixture well into the center of the mold and to smooth the top level. Cover with a piece of parchment paper and the lid, and freeze until very firm, 9-12 hours. Meanwhile, make the chocolate triangles.

2 MAKE THE CHOCOLATE TRIANGLES

1 Cut the chocolate into large chunks. Chop them with the chef's knife, or in a food processor using the pulse button. Melt the chocolate in a bowl set in a saucepan half-filled with hot water and let cool. Cut a strip of parchment paper 8-inches long and 1-inch wide. Spread the cooled, melted chocolate on the paper to an even layer about $\frac{1}{16}$-inch thick. Let cool until on the point of setting.

2 With the chef's knife, mark the strip of chocolate into triangles without cutting the paper. Or use a cookie cutter to form disks, crescents, or other shapes of your choice. For a curved shape, lift the strip of paper onto a rolling pin. Let set.

! TAKE CARE !
Do not refrigerate the chocolate shapes before they are set, or they will shrink away from the paper and buckle.

3 When the chocolate is firm, lift the paper away from the work surface, then carefully peel the chocolate away from the paper, using the metal spatula to slide between paper and chocolate. Handle the shapes as little as possible so the chocolate does not melt and become dull.

3 MAKE THE CHOCOLATE FUDGE SAUCE

1 Chop the chocolate. Put the water into a heavy-based saucepan. Add the chocolate and heat, stirring, until the chocolate has melted.

2 Dice the butter and add to the saucepan, then add the brown sugar. Bring to a boil, stirring so the ingredients are well mixed.

3 Simmer, stirring occasionally, until thick, 5-7 minutes. Stir in a pinch of salt and keep the sauce warm while you unmold the bombe.

4 UNMOLD AND DECORATE THE BOMBE

1 Whip the cream with the granulated sugar until stiff peaks form (see box, page 120). Fill the pastry bag with the sweetened whipped cream. Set aside.

Fold top of pastry bag over your hand so it forms collar

Warm knife under hot running water, then wipe dry before running knife around side of mold

3 Remove the lid and parchment paper. Dry the base of the mold and run a knife around the side of the bombe.

When bombe is loosened, ice cream melts a little

2 Take the mold from the freezer. Dip the mold in a bowl of cool water for 30-60 seconds to loosen the bombe.

4 Set a chilled serving plate on top of the mold and invert them, holding them firmly together.

ANNE SAYS
"If the bombe sticks, hold a hot damp cloth against the mold for several seconds."

Make sure serving plate is chilled

5 Lift the mold straight up and off the bombe. Wipe the plate to remove any melted ice cream. In hot weather, return the bombe to the freezer.

HOW TO WHIP AND SWEETEN CREAM AND MAKE CHANTILLY CREAM

Heavy cream, with a minimum 36% butterfat content, is best for whipping, and it should be thoroughly chilled. Chantilly cream is whipped cream flavored with sugar and vanilla, brandy, rum, or a liqueur such as Grand Marnier. Whipped cream can be covered and refrigerated up to 4 hours. It may separate slightly but will re-combine if whipped briefly.

! TAKE CARE !
If the cream is to be piped for decoration, take care not to overwhip it because the cream will be worked further when forced through the pastry bag. If too stiff, it will separate.

1 Pour the heavy cream into a chilled medium-sized bowl set in a larger bowl of ice water.

2 Whip until the cream forms soft peaks.

3 Add the sugar, and for Chantilly cream, the flavoring, and whip until the cream forms soft peaks again and just holds its shape.

Cream will soften slightly when sugar is added

Whisk will leave clear marks in cream

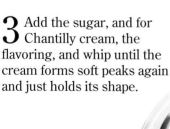

4 For stiff peaks, continue whipping until the whisk leaves clear marks in the cream.

! TAKE CARE !
If overwhipped, the cream will separate and turn to butter. When this is about to happen, it looks granular.

6 Pipe a ring of sweetened whipped cream rosettes around the base of the bombe.

ANNE SAYS
"For a few moments, the bombe will frost with moisture after unmolding, but this will evaporate by the time the bombe is ready to serve."

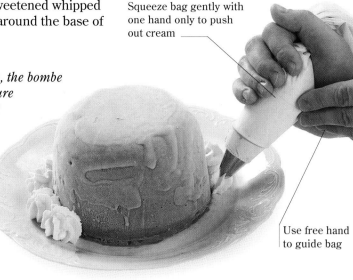

Squeeze bag gently with one hand only to push out cream

Use free hand to guide bag

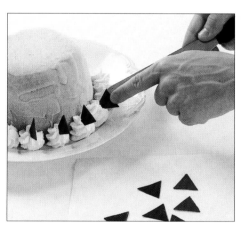

7 When the ring of rosettes is complete, pick up the chocolate triangles, using the metal spatula, and tip one into the center of each rosette. If you like, arrange slices of canned apricots around edge of plate.

Apricot slices add color and complement filling

Warm fudge sauce is optional

¶⊙¶ TO SERVE
Cut the bombe into wedges. Put the wedges on chilled individual plates and serve the warm fudge sauce separately.

V A R I A T I O N
BOMBE ROYALE

1 Make full quantity of Chocolate Ice Cream (see page 106).
2 Cut 1 lb homemade or store-bought jelly roll (preferably filled with apricot jelly) into 1/4-inch-thick slices.
3 Halve the slices and use to line the bottom and side of the mold, fitting them together as tightly as possible so there are no gaps. Chop the leftover pieces and place in a bowl.
4 Mix together 6 tbsp orange juice and 3 tbsp apricot brandy. Brush the jelly-roll lining with this mixture. Mix the remainder with the chopped jelly roll to moisten. Put the mold in the freezer until the jelly roll is firm.
5 Spoon the ice cream into the lined mold and slightly hollow out the center. Put the chopped jelly roll in the center and cover with more ice cream. Freeze until firm.
6 Unmold bombe as directed and pipe whipped cream rosettes on top and around base. Decorate with chocolate fans (see page 104) if you like.

—— GETTTING AHEAD ——
The bombe can be made and stored in the freezer up to 1 week. The chocolate triangles can be layered with parchment paper and stored in the refrigerator up to 1 week. Refrigerate the fudge sauce in a covered container and reheat it in a water bath. Whip the cream, unmold the bombe, and decorate it just before serving.

CHOCOLATE KNOW-HOW

Chocolate is made from the bean of the cacao tree. The beans are made into a thick paste through a process of drying, roasting, and grinding. The paste is "conched," or compressed by rollers, to make it smooth and mellow. The flavor of the chocolate depends on the selection of beans and how they are processed.

TYPES OF CHOCOLATE

The two main components of chocolate are cocoa solids and a light yellow fat called cocoa butter. Different types of block chocolate contain different proportions of the two, together with flavorings and sugar. The finest block chocolate always contains a high proportion of cocoa butter, on average 35 per cent, though it can be as high as 50 per cent. In inferior types of chocolate, vegetable oils or shortening may be substituted for cocoa butter.

Because the different types of chocolate give different results during cooking, it is important to use the type specified in the recipe.

SEMISWEET, PLAIN OR BITTERSWEET CHOCOLATE

This type of chocolate contains enough sugar to make it good to eat alone. This is the type most commonly used in cooking. The amounts of cocoa butter and flavoring vary enormously from brand to brand, so it is worth experimenting until you find the one that you prefer.

UNSWEETENED, BAKING OR BITTER CHOCOLATE

This chocolate contains no sugar at all. It can be hard to find so I use it only when strictly necessary.

WHITE CHOCOLATE

White chocolate contains cocoa butter (the amount depends on the brand) but because it has no cocoa solids, white chocolate must be labeled "white coating" in the U.S. Be sure to read the label because cheap imitations of white chocolate are common, and will list palm oil or shortening, rather than cocoa butter, as the primary ingredient.

MILK CHOCOLATE

In this type of chocolate, dried milk, or sometimes condensed milk, replaces some of the cocoa solids, producing a sweeter taste. Milk chocolate is more sensitive to heat and a bit harder to work with, so it is less commonly used in cooking and garnishing. I've used it in a few recipes where I want to create a contrast of taste and color with semisweet chocolate.

COCOA POWDER

This is pure unsweetened chocolate from which much of the cocoa butter has been extracted. Dutch-process or alkalized cocoa is the best as its flavor is mild and it dissolves easily. Cocoa is often used for giving cakes and desserts a light dusting of chocolate, particularly where there is a creamy filling, and for adding to basic mixtures.

Sweetened cocoa, also called powdered chocolate, may have powdered milk added and is often used for drinks. Do not confuse it with the unsweetened cocoa I use in my recipes.

COVERING CHOCOLATE

Often called dipping chocolate, coating chocolate, or couverture, this has a high cocoa butter content. It is available in semisweet, white and milk chocolate varieties. This is chef's chocolate, ideal for dipping because the high cocoa butter content means it melts easily and smoothly, and produces decorations with a high gloss.

STORING CHOCOLATE

Ideally chocolate should be kept cool at around 60° F in a dry, airy place. If chocolate is refrigerated, keep it in the vegetable drawer. Seal opened chocolate tightly from humidity and store it away from ingredients with strong odors. In good conditions, dark chocolate can be kept three months or more, longer than the white or milk chocolates that contain a high proportion of milk solids. Chocolate decorations can be refrigerated or frozen for a week or two, once they are set. If poorly stored, chocolate can develop a whitish film of cocoa butter or sugar. The film looks unattractive, but does not affect flavor.

WORKING WITH CHOCOLATE

With just a few simple chocolate techniques, you can create a wide variety of fillings, sauces, and decorations. All of these techniques are pictured in detail in individual recipes.

CHOPPING AND GRATING CHOCOLATE

When chopping or grating, it is important that the chocolate is firm, so on a warm day refrigerate it first. If you are chopping by hand, touch the chocolate as little as possible and be sure the chopping board is dry, because any moisture can affect the melting consistency of the chocolate.

To chop by hand: With a large chef's knife, chop the chocolate using the broad end, not the tip, of the blade.

To chop in a food processor: Cut the chocolate into small chunks and chop it using the pulse button. Do not overwork the chocolate or the heat of the machine can melt it. If necessary, process the chocolate in several batches.

To grate chocolate: Hold it firmly with a piece of foil or parchment paper and work it against the coarsest grid of the grater. Let the grated chocolate fall onto a sheet of parchment paper or a plate.

MELTING CHOCOLATE

There are a number of methods for melting chocolate. It is important that the container is uncovered and dry because any water or steam that comes in contact with the chocolate will cause it to seize or harden (see below right).

First, chop the chocolate in chunks of about the same size. A double boiler is good for melting chocolate, or you can set a metal or glass bowl in a pan of water (a water bath). The water should be hot but not simmering. You can also put the chopped chocolate on an ovenproof plate, then melt it over a pan of simmering water.

Once the chocolate starts to melt, stir it occasionally until melted and smooth, then take it from the heat. If the chocolate does seize, stir in vegetable shortening or oil one teaspoon at a time until the chocolate is smooth again. Some cooks prefer to melt chocolate in a microwave oven. Medium power is recommended and timing depends on your microwave oven and the type and amount of chocolate. For instance, two ounces of chopped semisweet chocolate takes about two minutes on Medium power.

TEMPERING CHOCOLATE

Tempering melted chocolate makes it more malleable and shiny for decorations. Covering chocolate (couverture) is the type most often used for tempering because it has a high cocoa butter content and achieves the greatest gloss.

Melt the chocolate in the top of a double boiler or in a bowl set in a water bath. Heat gently over hot but not simmering water, stirring with a wooden spoon until the chocolate is very smooth and reaches 115°F on a candy thermometer, five to seven minutes. Set the bowl of melted chocolate in a bowl of cool (not ice) water. Stir the chocolate often until it cools to 80°F, three to five minutes. Then set the chocolate over the pan of hot water again and heat it to 90°F. It is now ready to use.

PIPING CHOCOLATE

Disposable paper piping cones are useful for piping small amounts of chocolate.

To make two piping cones, fold an 8-inch x 14-inch rectangle of parchment paper in half diagonally and cut along the fold. Fold the short side of one triangle over to the right-angled corner to form a cone shape. Holding the cone together with one hand, wrap the long point of the triangle around the paper cone. Tuck the point of paper inside the cone to secure it. Repeat with the remaining triangle of paper to make another cone.

Fill one cone with melted, cooled chocolate and fold the top to seal. If you need a second cone, fill it with chocolate, seal, and keep it in a warm place so the chocolate does not set.

If piping directly on a cake or dessert, first snip the tip of the paper cone with scissors. Using light pressure, pipe the design or lettering in an even motion. For instructions on piping separate designs, look at the section on chocolate decorations (see page 124).

! TAKE CARE !

If chocolate is not carefully handled, it will separate or "seize," suddenly turning into a thick rough mass. This can be corrected by stirring in one to two teaspoons of vegetable oil or shortening until the chocolate becomes smooth again.
If melted chocolate comes into contact with a small amount of liquid or steam, it will seize.
If you try to melt chocolate over too small a quantity of liquid, it may seize.
All other ingredients should be at a similar temperature when mixed with melted chocolate. Adding a hotter liquid can cause the chocolate to seize, while cold liquid can make it lumpy.
Chocolate will scorch or seize if it is overheated during melting.

CHOCOLATE DECORATIONS

Melted chocolate can be transformed into many different shapes that can be used to decorate cakes and desserts of all kinds. Chocolate can also be piped into scrolls, fans, or lattices, or used for dipping fruit and nuts. Before trying these decorations, be sure to consult the information on working with chocolate on page 123.

MAKING CHOCOLATE LEAVES

Choose pliable leaves with deep veins, such as rose or ficus. Using a pastry brush or your fingertip, spread cooled melted chocolate on the shiny side of each leaf in a thin even layer, leaving a little of the stem exposed so the leaf can be peeled off easily. Set the leaves on a plate and let cool, then refrigerate until set. With the tips of your fingers, peel each leaf away from the chocolate. Handle the chocolate leaves as little as possible so they do not melt or become dull.

MAKING A CHOCOLATE RIBBON

A chocolate ribbon is a broad strip of chocolate that can be wrapped around an iced cake for an elegant presentation. Cut a strip of parchment paper as wide as the cake is high and long enough to wrap around the cake, allowing a little overlap. (For a glossy ribbon, the chocolate should be tempered.) Brush the paper strip with cooled, melted chocolate, spreading it in an even layer about a sixteenth-of-an-inch thick. Immediately wrap the ribbon around the cake, paper side out. Refrigerate until the chocolate is set, about one hour, then gently peel back the paper.

MAKING CHOCOLATE CURLS

Short curls of chocolate are a quick and easy topping for cakes and desserts. The chocolate should be at room temperature (about 70° F) so that it is easy to shape. Covering chocolate is the easiest to work with, although semisweet, milk, or white chocolate can also be used. Hold a block of chocolate at an angle and, with a vegetable peeler, shave away curls of chocolate. Work over a plate or piece of paper, so that the curls can be transferred to the dessert easily, without breaking or melting in your hands.

MAKING CHOCOLATE ROUNDS, SQUARES OR TRIANGLES

Spread melted chocolate evenly with a metal spatula in a sixteenth-of-an-inch layer over a strip of parchment paper. Leave to cool until on the point of setting. For rounds, whether small coins, or larger disks, use a round cookie cutter or the top of a glass to cut the shapes. For triangles, when on the point of setting, mark the chocolate with a knife without cutting through the paper. Make squares in the same way, cutting the chocolate with a knife when on the point of setting. For all shapes, once the chocolate has been cut, leave it on the paper until fully set, then carefully peel the chocolate away from the paper using a metal spatula.

PIPING CHOCOLATE DECORATIONS

Rather than piping designs freehand, you will find it easier to draw or trace them first in dark pen on a sheet of paper. Then place a piece of nonstick parchment paper on top so the design shows through, and fasten the papers to the counter top with sticky tape.

Snip the tip of the paper cone with scissors. Using light pressure, pipe melted chocolate on to the paper, following the outline of your drawing, letting the chocolate fall evenly from the tip without forcing it. Leave the shapes to set at room temperature. Once set, remove the decorations carefully with a metal spatula, handling them as little as possible so the chocolate does not melt or become dull.

CHOCOLATE-DIPPED FRUIT AND NUTS

Fresh, dried, or candied fruits such as sliced banana, cherries, and strawberries dipped in melted chocolate look very pretty arranged around the edge of a cake or dessert, or grouped together in clusters in the center.

The larger-shaped nut varieties can be hand-dipped in chocolate, too, and used as a decoration.

HOW-TO BOXES

Some basic techniques are general to a number of recipes; they are shown in extra detail in these special "How-to" boxes:

INDEX

126

ACKNOWLEDGMENTS

Photographer David Murray
Photographer's Assistant Jules Selmes

Chef Laurent Terrasson
Cookery Consultant Linda Collister
Home Economist Annie Nichols

US Editor Jeanette Mall
Indexer Sally Poole

Typesetting Rowena Feeny
Text film by Disc To Print (UK) Limited

Production Consultant Lorraine Baird

*Anne Willan would like to thank her
chief editor Cynthia Nims and associate
editor Kate Krader for their vital help
with writing the book and researching
and testing the recipes, aided by
La Varenne's chefs and trainees.*